Stitched Textile Landscapes

Kathleen Matthews

First published in Great Britain 2013

Search Press Limited
Wellwood, North Farm Road,
Tunbridge Wells, Kent TN2 3DR

ISBN: 978-1-84448-720-2

Suppliers
If you have difficulty in obtaining
any of the materials and equipment
mentioned in this book, then please
visit the Search Press website for
details of suppliers:
www.searchpress.com

Printed in China

Close-up detail of the trees in the Deer panel from my Misty
and Music quilt.

Contents

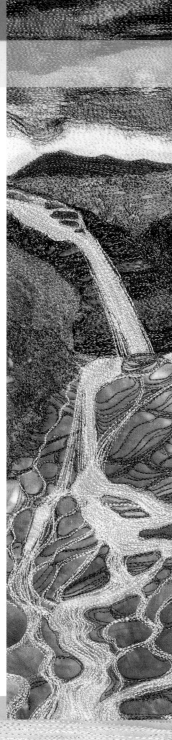

Introduction 6

Materials 8

Design 16

Dyeing 22

Transferring the design 30

Basic techniques 31

Elements of the landscape 40

Skies 40

Water 44

Trees & woodlands 48

Hills & mountains 52

Flowers in the landscape 54

Distance 58

Foregrounds 60

Fields & grasses 62

Rocks & pebbles 64

Buildings in the landscape 66

The seasons 68

Spring 68

Summer 70

Autumn 72

Winter 74

PROJECTS 76

Autumn Woodland 78

Flower Garden 88

Mountain Lake 98

Sunset Loch 108

Lavender Farm 118

Index 128

Introduction

Teaching textiles has been my career, my hobby and my pleasure; I have constantly studied to update my skills, and tried new products and materials as they appear. I now concentrate on creating textile landscapes. Every landscape I work is a new challenge; each one needs to be stitched differently to create the appearance of a three-dimensional picture from two-dimensional materials. In this book I have tried to convey some of my training from art college as well as inspirations that have influenced my work throughout the years.

I was born and bred in Britain, in the Forest of Dean, Gloucestershire; a beautiful wooded area between the River Severn and the River Wye. It has a very diverse landscape with hills, forest, fields, small lakes and far-reaching views. Every day has its own beauty, and as a result I find that I am constantly inspired by nature's diversity.

Photography has opened my eyes to the wonders of the world, and to the fact that every country has extraordinary scenery. I look with awe at photographic and travel books, and also watch travel documentaries on television. I have loved taking photographs from a young age. The invention of the digital camera has transformed photography; they are so quick and I can even take pictures through the car windscreen when I am a passenger. I try to have my camera with me at all times and I take photographs at every opportunity, to use in my stitched landscapes.

I have worked with fabrics and fibres throughout my career, teaching textiles to children from as young as six years old, to adults in their eighties, from City and Guilds textile and design subjects to leisure classes. I really enjoy the enthusiasm and the feedback from everyone.

I love to study fabrics: I find the colour, design, texture and feel of them therapeutic. Technology has transformed the fabric and thread industries. There is such a choice of fibres that are made into fantastic fabrics for all occasions. There is an array of beautiful threads in an amazing colour palette and a multitude of textures, which is fantastic for stitched landscapes.

Landscapes are a great subject, regardless of the time of year or of day, and whatever the weather. Every landscape is a challenge. Study the landscape you want to create carefully, paying attention to detail and to the choice of materials you will use. Texture, colour, light, shade and shape are extremely important.

I prefer to dye my own fabrics using space-dyeing techniques with procion dyes. This method achieves a multitude of unusual colours, shades, and textural effects and will give you wonderful fabrics for your stash cupboard, ready for future landscapes. If you do not wish to dye your own fabrics, you can buy a huge range of hand-dyed, printed and batik fabrics that can give you a similar effect.

I have been asked many times when I will write a book showing the techniques I use in my work. At long last I have achieved my ambition and have found time. I hope you will enjoy reading this book and trying out my ideas, and that you will start to design and stitch your own textile landscapes.

One Moment in Time

This is my interpretation of this beautiful cove in Barbados. It was made with my torn strip technique (see page 32). There is lots of detail in the foreground, with little houses and large villas among the palm trees. The houses were appliquéd with fusible web. The middle distance shows hillsides covered in trees and vegetation, cliffs and coves. There are hills in the far distance, and, behind the long, thin strip of land you can see the deep blue of the ocean. The main area of water was made from vivid blue, green and purple organza, accented with metallic organza, and the wave crests were stitched with white viscose and silver metallic thread. The amazing white sands were made from very pale natural calico cotton, appliquéd in place with fusible web because of the thin fine lines of sand going out into the sea. The wet edges of the sand were stitched with a darker shade of beige, with white stitching for the surf and waves. The sky was made from blue and white torn strips of space-dyed cotton, which was then heavily machine stitched.

Materials

Dyeing equipment

Dyeing fabrics yourself is very satisfying. You will achieve a selection of wonderful coloured fabrics that are totally unique in colour and pattern, and that will enhance your stitched landscapes enormously.

There is very little specialist equipment required when you dye your fabrics at home with this method. You should be able to source all you need or viable alternatives from your kitchen, except for the cold water dye, a face mask and maybe soda. The dyeing techniques are shown on pages 22–29.

Shown here, clockwise from top left are:

Kitchen scales for weighing the salt and soda.
A salt solution and a soda solution stored in separate clean, screw-top containers.
A plastic cat litter tray (or a similar container) in which to dye the fabric.
Two jugs to mix salt and soda solutions.
Cooking salt.
Washing soda.
An apron to protect your clothes.
Rubber gloves to protect your hands.
Tablespoons for measuring when making salt and soda solutions.
Teaspoons to measure dye powder.
A face mask to stop you inhaling the dye powder.
Three cold-water procion dyes, sold in pots or sachets. Red, yellow and blue are good for your first try at dyeing.
Three jars in which to mix the dyes.
Non-biological washing liquid for hand washing fabrics.
Sticks to stir the dye solution.
A saucer and peg used for the burn test shown on page 28, to find out whether or not a fabric is pure cotton.

You will also need old newspapers to protect your work surfaces.

Opposite
A selection of the fabrics I have dyed myself.

Fabrics

There are so many fabrics available, made from natural fibres such as cotton and silk or synthetic fibres like organza and chiffon, or a mixture of both like polyester/cotton. Fabric can be transparent, have a textured surface, a smooth, flat weave, an open weave like scrim or a piled surface such as velvet. I work mainly with cotton and organza fabrics although I would not dismiss any fabric without careful consideration, as it may be the very piece I will need for future work. Most of the time I use my own space-dyed fabrics: smooth-weave cotton and open-weaved scrim and muslin.

Cotton is a natural, very versatile fibre, woven into many fabrics. Different weaves and weights are available, from very thin fine gauze or crêpe made into bandages, to heavy brocade curtaining. I use a lot of cotton fabric, in the light to medium weight range. Cottons are readily available from dress fabric and craft shops, and there are also specialist shops, which sell cotton fabric prepared for dyeing. Cotton is easily dyed, very easy to stitch by hand or machine, and available in many widths. If the cotton fabric has not been pre-shrunk, it is advisable to wash well before use to remove any dressing in the fabric.

The fabrics I use are as follows:

Fine turban cotton, a lovely soft fine cotton fabric that dyes well and is easy to handle.

Muslin and cheesecloth are both very fine, loosely woven cotton fabric, easy to dye and distress for surface texture.

Cotton lawn, a very fine, soft, smooth, closely woven cotton.

Dress fabrics and patchwork fabric in a medium-weight cotton, suitable for the base and background fabric, as well as for appliquéd areas.

Calico is another very useful cotton fabric, mainly for sale in its natural cream colour, although bleached calico is also available.

Finely woven cotton sheeting is very useful, not just for its size, but also because it dyes beautifully and is easy to use.

Novelty weaves: knitted and velvet cotton fabrics can be useful for textured areas on your pictures.

Scrim is a very open, fine-weave cotton. I use it often for texture as it will gather and you can distress it and pull threads out easily or use it scrunched up and stitched on to a landscape. It dyes extremely well.

Polyester/cotton mixes are useful as only the cotton thread will dye, creating a lighter effect.

Organza is made mainly from polyester, in a multitude of colours and effects. It gives life and light to landscapes, though the downside is that it frays badly. Sheer organza has a plain weave and is good for overlaying. Crystal organza is slightly thicker and has a sparkly look. Shot organza has two colours woven together, one in the warp and the other in the weft. As the fabric moves, you can see the different colours. Shaded organza is dyed in different shades of one colour, usually light to dark down the width of the fabric. Rainbow organza is dyed with areas of different colours down the width of the the fabric, for instance red, purple, blue, green, yellow and orange – hence the name. It is also dyed in other colours. Metallic organza is woven with a metallic thread. Printed organza can be useful as you will have various colours in one piece. Silk organza can be dyed or bought ready coloured. There are many variations on the types mentioned above, which may be sold as dress or soft furnishing fabric. I always buy a piece of organza when I find a new colour, texture or interwoven type.

Chiffon is a very soft, semi-opaque fabric. It is not easy to buy by the metre, but it can be found in evening wear sections of fabric shops and in Indian fabric shops. Chiffon scarves are available in many colours and in a much finer, semi-sheer fabric. Scarves can be bought in one colour or shaded, as well as printed. Look in charity or second-hand shops for cheaper options.

Viscose is an opaque, fine-weave, soft handling fabric. It does not fray much so is useful for shadows and light areas. Indian fabric shops are a good source of long viscose scarves.

Many other fabrics such as silk velvet, cotton velvet, silk and viscose velvet and also net and tulle can also be used in landscapes.

Wadding (batting)

There are many different waddings on the market: polyester, cotton, bamboo, silk or wool, as well as combinations of these fibres. I use a white or natural cotton wadding which has no glue additions, instead it has been needle punched with hundreds of needles into a fine base fabric. This gives me stability, allowing me to machine stitch heavily without any distortion or disintegration of the wadding. The needle punching process stops any threads or fibres from bearding through to the right side of my work. I find it very easy to control the movement of my work under the machine needle when stitching, even on large pieces of work, because the wadding creates stability, so I do not need to use a hoop. Cotton wadding gives a slight lift to your work, and I really like this effect. Always work from the middle outwards, otherwise you may end up with too much or not enough fabric at the centre of your work.

Because the wadding is cotton, there is some shrinkage, usually five per cent. If you intend to launder your work at a later date, it may be advantageous to wash the wadding first to avoid shrinkage later. I don't shrink my wadding because I frame my landscape pictures and cover them with glass to protect them from dust.

Clockwise from top left: turquoise organza, royal blue sheer organza, gold and blue striped soft furnishing organza, striped, coloured metallic organza, blue/pink shot organza, blue metallic organza, burnt orange sheer organza, lilac and cerise pink sheer organza, orange, green and purple shaded organza, royal blue, green and yellow chiffon scarves, orange crystal organza, white and cream cottons in different weights, crêpe bandage, cotton lace, polyester/cotton, scrim, viscose, cotton velvet, viscose velvet, silk velvet, silk chiffon, silk ready for dyeing, acid green, pink and red chiffon scarves; pink, beige, mauve and dark green viscose scarves, orange organza, green and yellow shot organza, orange and cerise organza with metallic stripes.

Threads

I use viscose and rayon machine-embroidery thread because of its lustre; the shine enhances any fabric. It is produced in an amazing number of colours, as well as shades and tones of each colour; one manufacturer has a 360-colour range. Viscose thread can be bought as a solid colour or random mixtures of colours. I buy by colour rather than manufacturer but I do test the strength first before committing myself to buying more threads.

Metallic machine thread can be purchased in several shades of gold and silver as well as coloured metallic. I use it for stitching areas in water to give the reflection and sparkle of light.

Six-strand hand embroidery thread can be divided into six individual strands. This means that you can work French knots, for example, in anything between one and six strands to achieve different-sized stitches (see the small flower picture on page 54). This is ideal if you want to portray distance in a landscape. This thread is easy to use for hand embroidery.

Cotton perle is a non-divisible twisted thread for hand embroidery. It is available in several thicknesses and many colours.

Tapestry wool is a 4-ply wool that is non-divisible and can be used for hand embroidery.

Crewel wool is a 2-ply non-divisible hand embroidery thread.

Tacking cotton is a fine fluffy thread made specially for temporary stitching. It is available in several colours. I prefer white, which is sold on large reels. It is easy to remove but will not fall out of the fabric if you need to cut the thread at intervals while machine stitching.

Sewing equipment

You will need an electric sewing machine with straight and zigzag stitch and the ability to drop the dogteeth or a plate to cover the dogteeth. You also need a free machine embroidery foot to fit your machine. Take care of your machine; the fluff from cotton wadding will clog the bobbin compartment and the dogteeth, so make sure you clean the machine regularly and oil it if required. Stitching through many layers of fabric will blunt your machine needles, so change your needle as required.

Below is my basic sewing kit:
Cutting shears with large blades for cutting out fabric.
Embroidery hoops with the inner ring wrapped with white cotton tape, to hold the fabric taut while you hand embroider.
Tape measure to measure your fabrics.
Long glass-headed pins to pin fabrics in place. Glass heads are better than plastic, as they will not melt if you accidentally place a hot iron on them.
Scissors with small, pointed blades to enable you to cut out very small pieces of fabric and to cut around intricate parts of patterns.
Sewing machine bobbins. You will need at least three so that you can fill them with your bobbin thread when you start to machine stitch. This will enable you to replace the bobbin when it runs out of thread, without needing to rewind bobbins constantly.
Selection of crewel needles and sharps. Crewel needles have a long eye, which will enable you to thread the needle with several strands of embroidery thread or thicker threads. Sharps have small round eyes, suitable for finer threads such as machine threads.
Quick unpick; essential for unpicking stitching that is not required.
Small, hooked scissors, very useful for picking up and cutting fraying threads.
Thimble to protect your finger from getting sore.
Small, sharp-pointed scissors; very useful to cut into small areas.
Machine embroidery needles, sometimes called metallic needles. These have elongated eyes which help to prevent the fraying and stripping of machine metallic thread and embroidery threads.

Embellishments

I used organza ribbons in red, green, white and pale blue. This is more economical than buying a large piece of organza fabric. Ribbons were used for sunsets, water and autumn tints in some of the pictures.

Blue and white textured knitting yarn and white, fringed novelty knitting yarn were used on the water pieces (see top right and pages 65 and 117).

Sections from the white lace shown below were used on the Flower Garden project on page 93 to depict the white flowers in the centre of the picture (see right).

Natural cotton lace can be used as it is or dyed. Space-dyed cotton lace was used for the Lace Lavender Fields piece on page 55 (see below, right).

Narrow black ribbon was used for the Sunset Loch project shown on pages 114–115 (see right, second from bottom).

Small, black glass beads were used to create the poppy centres in the Poppy Fields piece on page 71 (see right, bottom).

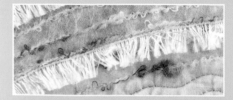

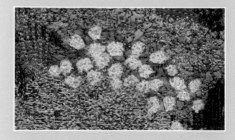

Knitting yarns.

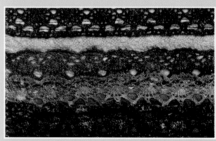

White lace.

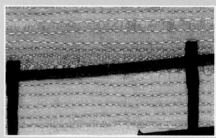

Space-dyed cotton lace.

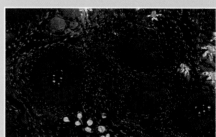

Ribbon.

Beads.

14

Other materials

Right:
Mini craft iron to press small or difficult areas and to attach small pieces of fusible web appliqué.
Steam iron to iron all fabrics including the space-dyed fabrics, and for attaching fusible web appliqué.

Bottom picture, top row left to right:
Large transparent ruler to enable you to see your work whilst measuring and lining up areas.
Baking parchment to be placed beneath and on top of work while you heat the fusible web appliqué pieces with the iron.
Black L shapes to place on your work to see how it looks in a frame.
Double mountboard frame, to frame your work when it is finished.
Light box for tracing the design.

Middle row left to right:
A4 white paper for patterns and sketching.
Clear sticky tape to join patterns and designs together.
Masking tape to attach photographs and design work so that they can be removed later.
HB pencils for design work and writing notes.
Sketchbooks for sketching, design drawings, paintings and details.
Eraser to remove pencil marks.
Paintbrushes in various sizes to paint colour into sketches.
Watercolour paints to colour drawings.
Pastel fixative to stop the pastels from flaking and transferring to the fabric.
Paint mixing palette to enable you to mix the watercolour paints.
Metal ruler with raised finger groove; if you decide to cut with a craft knife this will stop you cutting your fingers.

Bottom row, left to right:
Paper scissors with sharp points for cutting out patterns.
Soft pastels for colouring your designs and drawings.

Design

Finding inspiration

The natural world never fails to inspire me. Inspiration is all around me, whether I'm in my own garden or travelling in different countries. No landscape is the same; they all have their own interest and beauty, constantly changing from morning to night. How often have you been completely captivated by the amazing colours of a sunset? My work can be inspired by the beauty of a flower garden, the peace and tranquillity of a lake in a valley, surrounded by towering, majestic mountains or soft rolling hills, or a quiet, peaceful woodland or forest. Other parts of the world can be stark and barren, but this provides a contrast and the overall effect is beautiful and fascinating to me.

Using photographs

Photographs are very useful when designing or creating a textile landscape. Your own photograph will be unique. With the telescopic lens feature on my camera, I take various long-distance pictures. When the landscape is wide, I take several shots to make up a panoramic view when the photographs are joined together. I also take close-up pictures of any foreground interest so that I have a very good record of the landscape. Study your photographs either on a computer screen or as prints. Choose the ones you are interested in and feel you would like to develop into a textile landscape. Do not make a final decision now – review them again later, as you may change your mind on a second viewing. With a fresh look you may notice other elements you did not see before. Study details as well as the overall picture before making your choice.

Take stage by stage photographs during the construction of your stitched landscape, as these will be invaluable later as a record of how you stitched each section. Photographs will also give you a fresh eye on how your landscape looks and help you to identify if there are any problem areas.

These are some of the reference photographs I used for the stitched landscapes that appear as step-by-step demonstrations in this book; clockwise from top left: Flower Garden, page 88, Autumn Woodland, page 78, Lavender Farm, page 118, Sunset Loch, page 108 and Mountain Lake, page 98.

Using a photocopier

A photocopier is extremely useful, enabling you to enlarge your landscape photographs and make outline patterns. When I have decided on the photograph I wish to work with, I enlarge it up to A4 size in colour on the best photographic setting. The larger size enables me to look deeper into the landscape and see other interesting details. Some features can then be repositioned or removed while others can be added by photocopying, cutting and sticking in place. I use masking tape to attach new sections, as it allows me to reposition parts of the image until I am happy with the end result. You can of course use your computer for the design process, enlarging and joining images on screen and then printing as required. See page 30 for full instructions on how to transfer your chosen design.

The photocopy used in the design of the Flower Garden project on page 88.

Sketching

Sketching on site is a great help, recording detail, colour and texture. All you need to sketch your ideas is a pencil and a sketchbook. Jot down a few ideas to remind you later or make a scaled detailed drawing. Sketching will make you aware of every rise and fall in a landscape, and of shape, distance, colour and texture. The positions of buildings, trees, hedges or other important details give the landscape interest and recording these will enable you to create an exciting textile landscape. Draw the main lines first: the horizon, middle ground and foreground. This will help you to simplify what you see. Check angles in relation to one another, using your pencil held at arm's length as a guide. Draw in the main details in the distance, then the foreground detail. If the focal point has any detail that needs noting, do a close-up drawing of this. Add shadows and note the direction of the light source. Write down colours, either in position or on a chart. If you have watercolours or another colour medium, paint the individual colours. This will provide the most accurate record, as colour is extremely difficult to remember.

Composition

There are many rules on composition but I do not intend going into lengthy detail.
I use the following basic rules.

Rule of division by three

If a picture is divided into three equal
sections it is pleasing to the eye. The
main focal areas should be one-third
in, this can be from the sides, top or
bottom. Note that in the Mountain
Lake project (right and page 98), the
waterline is one-third up from the
bottom and the top of the mountain
is one-third down from the top of the
picture, creating a pleasing, peaceful
scene based on strong horizontal lines. In the Memories of Happy Days bluebell
wood picture (far right), the main focal area, the foreground tree trunk, is one-
third in from the right (see pages 86–87 for the full-sized image).

The main area of interest in the foreground should be off-centre

This might be a tree or a building, and if it is pictured off-centre, it makes
the picture much more interesting than if it is in the centre. Note how
the two compositions shown on the left have a tree (or a trunk) as the
focal point, and both appear slightly off-centre. The full-sized versions are
shown on pages 39 and 49.

The eye should follow naturally around the picture

Try to get the interest to circulate inside the picture and avoid definite exit points
that make the eye go off the edge. Note how the stream in the Through the Valley
picture on the right leads the eye into the heart of the composition. It would not
work nearly so well if it led the eye off at the left-hand side (see pages 106–107).

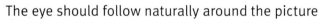

Create perspective

Linear elements such as fences, roads, hedges, and rows of houses or trees
help to create a feeling of depth and distance in your work. The general rule is
that lines above the eye line level travel down, and lines below the eye line level
travel up. Note how in this landscape featuring buildings (Naas House, page 126
and left) the path slopes upwards towards the eye level line, narrowing as it goes,
and the fence posts look tall in the foreground and shorter as they recede.

When choosing your composition, consider changing the dimensions of the
picture; maybe a long, thin section going down or across will be more dramatic,
or maybe just one small section from your reference photograph. Consider
various possibilities: a square, a rectangle, a narrow strip or a long section from
the original picture (see page 30, step 1).

Light source and shadows

It is very important to locate where the light is coming from in a scene, as this will help you to position all the shadows accurately, giving form and mass. Look for the shadows that identify where the light is coming from: the light source (the sun in a landscape) will be opposite the cast shadow. It is not always easy to work out the position of the light source when it is an overcast day, so you may need to imagine it, but you need to be consistent, and make sure the shadows are always on the correct side in your landscape picture.

Shadows give your landscape a three-dimensional look. A shadow can identify a sharp edge, changing immediately from light to dark, for example on a building or box. On a rounded edge such as a tree trunk, the shadows will graduate from light to dark. Remember a photograph is two-dimensional, but with the help of shadows we can produce work that appears three-dimensional. A good tip is to photocopy or print your photograph in monochrome – this will show where the light is concentrated.

Colours change in the light and shade, making your work more vibrant as well as creating depth. Shadows may look black, especially in photographs, but study them carefully, identifying any colours you can see. There will be a range of shades of the main colour from light to dark.

Shading

Try this exercise to help you understand how shading and shadows work. It will help you to construct the effect you want to achieve in your landscapes. Remember, anything you can draw with a pencil, you can stitch on your sewing machine.

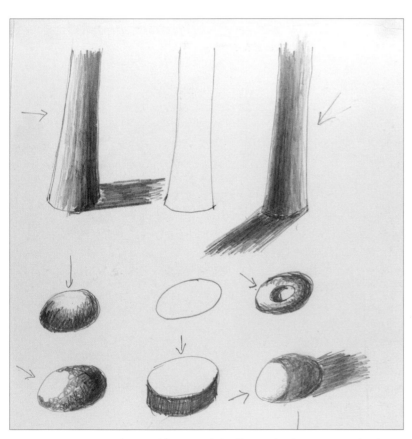

The drawing shows how shading can transform a flat two-dimensional shape into a three-dimensional shape. In the middle of the top row is a simple line drawing of a tree trunk. On the left of this is a shaded drawing showing the light source on the left, with light shading graduating to very dark shading on the right-hand side, leaving a very thin line of reflected light on the right-hand side of the trunk. The cast shadow is on the ground, exactly opposite the light source. In the drawing on the right, the light source is on the right behind the tree, (see arrow). The cast shadow on the ground is exactly opposite to it. A narrow line of reflected light is on the left-hand side.

In the centre of the middle row is a simple oval shape, the starting point for the other drawings. To the left of this is an oval shape with curved shading at the bottom, graduating upwards. This gives the impression of a solid, round shape. On the right is an oval shape with a second oval drawn in the centre. Shading on the outside makes the oval solid, and the shading on the inner oval makes it look hollow.

On the left of row three, the oval has dark shading on the right, graduating to lighter shading, which gives the impression of an egg or pebble shape. In the middle, the oval shape has a base added in dark shadow, giving the impression of a flat top and bottom. On the right, the shading of this oval shape has stopped in a circle shape on the left-hand side, which makes it look as if the section on the left is flat. The cast shadow is at the back.

Creating scenes in fabric and stitch

Choose your fabrics and threads carefully; colour, pattern and texture are very important and can enhance or be detrimental to the finished work. It is also important to try out different techniques to achieve the effect you need. When trying out techniques in this way, always use the fabric and threads you think you may use for the finished work, as all materials give different final results. Try different stitches on the machine and by hand to create the effects you want. Stitching can change shapes dramatically, giving depth, contours, edges and lots of details. Remember, any line you can draw with a pencil you can also make with a sewing machine or by hand embroidery.

I always use cotton wadding (batting) between the two layers of fabric when machine stitching, as this gives stability and eliminates the need to use an embroidery hoop, but for hand stitching I find that using a hoop helps.

Here I am trying out viscose thread colours for the sky in the landscape shown on page 39. This was my final choice: I used all four blues as well as white. Remember that when the thread is on the reel it will look darker, so to check that you have the best match, pull out a single strand from each reel, lay them on the fabric side by side, gradually start to close your eyes and the first thread to disappear, blending into the fabric, is the best colour match. Repeat with all your other threads.

Detail of the part-stitched sky, showing how the straight lines of machine stitching blend the different blue fabrics together, softening the hard edges by overlapping and allowing the first and second colours to intertwine.

Close-up detail of the huge oak tree, which stands in the centre of the rapeseed field. I used distressed green scrim, swirling it around to represent sections of the tree canopy and branches. I machine stitched into the scrim, adding light and shade, as well as more detail to the shape of the tree.

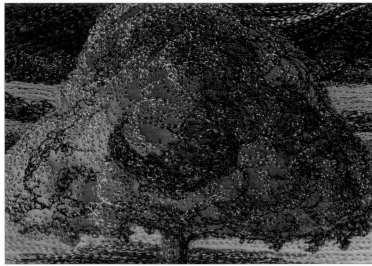

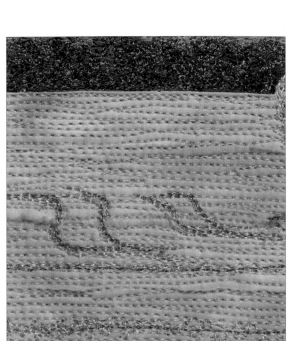

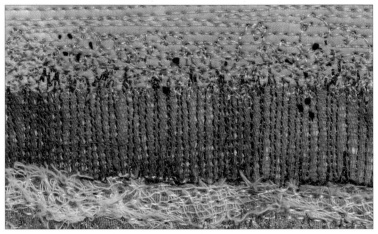

This close-up detail shows the straight stitching on the rapeseed field. The field is made from torn strips of yellow space-dyed cotton fabric, with the strips deepening in colour slightly as they come towards the foreground. These were then machine stitched in random horizontal lines. I also stitched the lines where the farmer had driven his tractor in the field to spray his crop. The tractor wheels have flattened some of the crop, causing shadows between the standing rapeseed. I machine stitched these lines in brown thread with a few grey stitches to emphasise some sections. The front lines were then stitched in beige thread in a circular movement to give depth to the flowers.

Detail of the edge of the rapeseed field. I tore a strip of green space-dyed muslin and laid it in position with the edge under the yellow field fabric, to represent the stalks of the rapeseed. I then added green space-dyed cotton for the foreground field, and placed a row of distressed dyed scrim on top, to look like dried cut grass. I machine stitched the stalks in straight vertical lines with a several different shades of green thread, working up and down, finishing at different heights to make it look more natural, with a few uneven stitches at the top to give the impression of several rows. The flowers at the front of the field were machine stitched with slightly darker yellow thread in small circular shapes. I repeated this with beige thread to create a second row of flowers further back. A few red poppies were stitched with French knots using one strand of red six-strand embroidery thread.

Detail of the gently rolling background hills. The blue sky becomes lighter at it goes behind the hills. The sun is shining from the left, giving bright light reflections on the left-hand slopes of the hills, with shadows on the right. The hills were cut from one piece of blue, green and purple space-dyed cotton fabric. The machine stitching in greens, mauves and purples emphasises the contours and shadows of the hills. A little white stitching at the top of the hills creates highlights, leaving small areas of the fabric colours and patterns showing through to give depth to the hills.

Dyeing

I like to dye my own fabrics as I feel I can get more individual and unusual colours and patterns this way. I like the individuality and excitement of not knowing exactly what you have created until you see the end result.

I use cold water procion dyes. Different fabrics and fibres can be dyed together in the same dye bath, including: natural fibres and threads, cotton, viscose and silk, as well as mixed natural and synthetic fabrics and threads.

The results cannot be repeated identically, although with practice you will be able to produce similar results. If you want to dye more fabric to the same colour, try weighing and measuring the exact amounts of dye and the fluids used, write down the exact recipe to refer to again and keep a sample of the dyed material produced.

For general rules on mixing colours, think back to school art lessons: red, yellow and blue are the primary colours, and the secondary colours are orange, green and purple. Mix red and yellow to make orange; blue and red to make purple; and red, yellow and blue mixed together will make a muddy brown. To achieve paler colours, use less dye powder or more water.

The method shown here achieves the maximum range of colours in one dye bath. The resultant dyed fabrics will be invaluable to place in your stash for future landscape projects. Procion dyes can be bought in a wide range of colours, either in small tins or packets or larger containers if you intend dyeing lots of fabric.

1 In one kitchen jug, mix a salt solution from 150g (5oz) of cooking salt in 0.6 litres (1 pint) of boiling water. In another, mix a soda solution from 110g (4oz) of washing soda with 0.6 litres (1 pint) of boiling water. Leave to cool, then store the two solutions in separate, labelled screw-top bottles.

You will need

Clean, wide-necked glass jars

Plastic stirrers or knitting needles for stirring dye

Rubber gloves

Old newspapers or plastic, to protect work surfaces

3 teaspoons and 2 tablespoons

Large cat litter trays, washing up bowls, plastic boxes, or any watertight container that will hold the fabric

150g (5oz) cooking salt

110g (4oz) washing soda

2 measuring jugs

Procion cold water dye in red, yellow and blue

Face mask

Apron or protective clothing

Non-biological washing liquid

White, cream or pale fabrics with a natural content: calico, cotton, viscose, crêpe, rayon, silk or cotton mix such as polyester/cotton

Threads and cotton lace

2 large plastic screw-top bottles

HEALTH AND SAFETY
Wear a mask, as dye particles can be harmful.
Cover all surfaces.
Do not use any bowls, spoons or other items for food after using them for dyeing.
Always wear rubber gloves or you will have multicoloured hands and the dye could be harmful to the skin.
Wear protective clothing to avoid dye spoiling your clothes.
Make sure you wash all surfaces and utensils thoroughly after all dyeing sessions.
If you wash and spin your dyed fabric in your washing machine and dry in the tumble dryer, wash the machines thoroughly or you may get multicoloured clothing when you do the next load.

Folded method

2 Wash, rinse and wring out all the fabrics to be dyed. Dye several fabrics at once; I have used calico, cotton, viscose and crêpe. Fold each piece of fabric in four or eight, or whatever will fit your receptacle. I have used a cat litter tray.

Threads

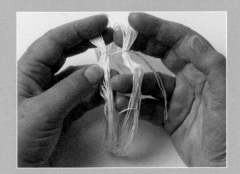

5 Skein any threads for dyeing. Take the skein and tie it loosely with a separate thread in a figure of eight as shown. Repeat in two other areas of the skein. Wash the thread.

8 Add 1 tablespoon (15ml) of the salt solution, then 2 tablespoons (30ml) of the soda solution to each jar, and stir well.

Scrunched method

3 In another cat litter tray I have used a selection of small pieces of 100% cotton, polyester/cotton, scrim, muslin and viscose. Scrunch them with your fingers one at a time into the tray. The pieces of fabric on the bottom may have less dye, so will have paler areas which are very useful for landscapes.

6 Place the threads and cotton lace in various areas of a cat litter tray between other fabrics to be dyed. This will give you different colourways along the threads and lace.

9 Top up each jar with cold water. If you are using a large jar, do not fill to the top, or the colour will be pale. Stir well.

Gathered method

4 Lay out the fabric over the edge of the tray. You can do this with any fabric; this is muslin. Starting at the bottom, pull the fabric into the tray and start gathering it with your fingers into little folds. If the fabric is too wide, gather the side edges too.

7 Wearing a mask and rubber gloves, place one heaped teaspoon of dye into each of three jars, in three different colours, using a clean spoon for each colour. I have used red, yellow and blue. Add a little warm water to each dye and stir with plastic stirrers.

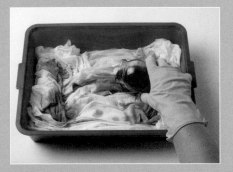

10 Make three or four indents in the fabric in one of the prepared cat litter trays, using your gloved hand. Spoon or pour the dyes into the indents, one colour at a time; I did the yellow first.

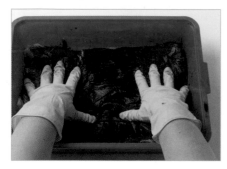

11 Make more indents and pour in the red and blue dyes. Always put in the palest dyes first, then darker, then darkest. Repeat in all the prepared trays. Press the fabrics down with your gloved hands to make sure the dyes combine. Lower layers may be paler; check by lifting a corner to see if the dye has penetrated. If it has not soaked through, pour some of the remaining dye underneath and press down again. Leave for at least thirty minutes.

12 Pour away the remaining dyes and wring out the fabric. Rinse the fabrics in cold water until the dye is removed and the water runs clear. Wash them, with the threads, in hot water with non-biological washing liquid. Rinse them in cold water.

13 Dry the dyed pieces and iron them to see what effects you have created before they are completely dry. Finally look at the different areas on your fabric; see the beautiful intricate patterns and the amazing colour palette you have achieved. There will be pure primary and secondary colours and lots of unusual shades and combinations where the colours have bled into one another

The cotton lace dyed here was used in this piece, also shown on page 55.

Trying different colour combinations

You could try several shades of blue dye together for sky and water; different greens, yellow and purples together or separately for hills, mountains, trees and land; and red, yellow and green for autumn tints.

Enjoy working with the unique fabrics that you have created; they are ideal for textile landscapes.

These 10cm (4in) squares are all cut from one piece of space-dyed cotton fabric. The white cotton was scrunch-dyed with only three colour dyes: red, yellow and blue. Where the colours of the dyes have combined, there are lots of secondary colours: greens, purples and oranges as well as many other shades and tones of each colour. The patterns achieved on each square are beautiful pictures in their own right, and ideal for use in stitched landscapes.

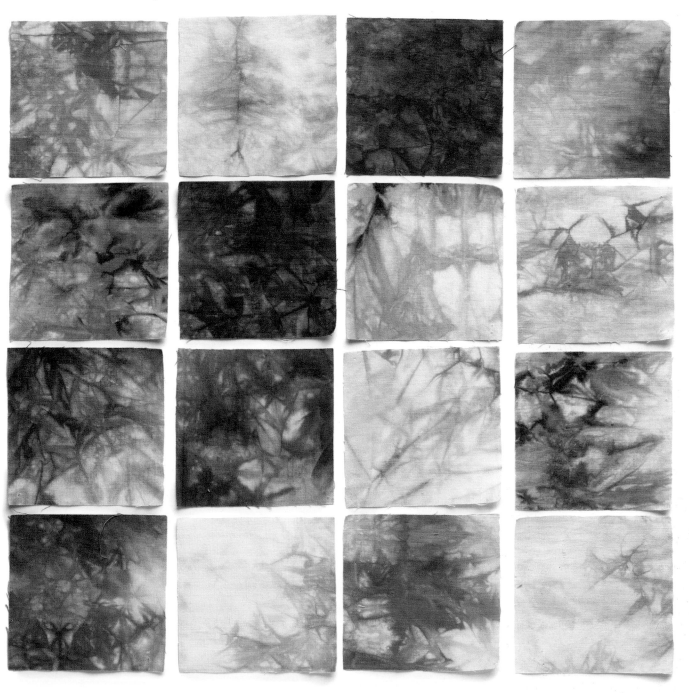

Dyed threads.

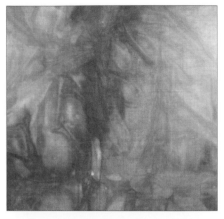

Dyed cotton lace.

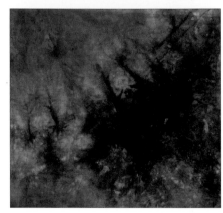

Fine cotton lawn, dyed using the folded method.

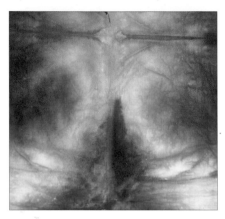

Cotton dyed using the folded method, showing the mirroring effect.

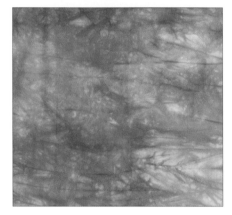

Cotton dyed using the scrunched method.

Another piece dyed using the scrunched method.

A piece dyed using the gathered method.

A long piece dyed using the gathered method and (below) more of the same piece.

A selection of dyed fabrics.

Dyeing different fabrics and threads

Choose fabrics and threads with a natural fibre content: cotton, viscose or silk.

Cotton fabric is the easiest to find and it is available in many weights from gauze and scrim, which are very fine, open-weave cottons to heavy and textured cottons.

Viscose fabric is not readily available, so I use Indian viscose scarves or ask in dress fabric shops. Viscose takes the dye extremely well, achieving very deep and vivid colours. If you want paler shades, mix dye with more water or use less dye powder.

Silk fabric will dye but usually in softer shades. It is available in different weights and textures, from very fine silk to textured dupion, as well as woven patterns.

Velvet made from cotton or viscose will dye beautifully, giving you deep, strong colours. Silk velvet tends to take paler shades with a lovely sheen.

Mixed fibres – natural fibres mixed with synthetic such as polyester/cotton – will dye paler because only the cotton content will take the colour. This can be very effective.

It is useful to know whether a fabric contains synthetic fibres. I have been sold fabric as 100% cotton which, when tested, proved to contain synthetic fibres. I now ask for a sample and do a burn test (shown below) to find out. Do not try this inside a building as you may set off the fire alarms of sprinklers. Shops usually have the fibre content marked on the label, but when buying elsewhere, the sellers do not always know the true fibre content.

Burn test

1 Cut a long thin piece of fabric, approximately 15 x 4cm (6 x 1½in). Hold the end with a peg or tongs, set fire to it with a match and hold it over a bowl of water in case it flares. If it does, you can drop it into the water to extinguish the flame. When the fabric is partially burnt, place it on a china saucer or plate and leave it to burn away. When it is cool, if you only have a fine grey ash left on the saucer, it is 100% cotton.

2 Repeat the test with another piece of fabric. If it burns with black smoke and leaves a sticky mess, which then hardens when cold to a small black globular substance, then it has some synthetic content.

A selection of dyed fabrics

Scrim, ironed.   Scrim, unironed.

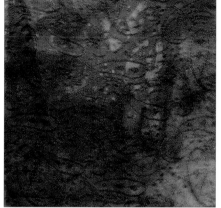

Patterned silk.

Viscose.

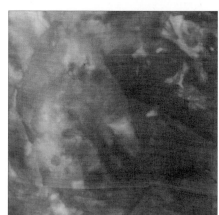

Habotai silk.

Dupion silk.

Silk chiffon.

Crêpe bandage.

Below: three different velvets.

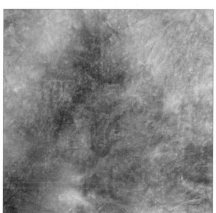

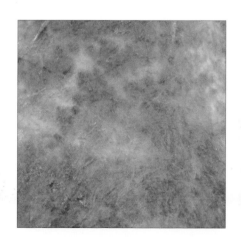

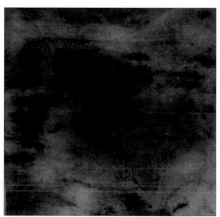

Transferring the design

On this page I have shown you how to work from a photograph, changing and simplifying the original by adding and taking away features to create a suitable design for a textile picture. This is called artistic license, and it has happened thoughout history. Even in the famous Hay Wain painting by Constable, the composition was changed from the original scene to create a more interesting painting.

1 Take your reference photograph and enlarge it. Here I have taken a small print and enlarged it to A4 size on the best photographic setting. Then experiment with different crops until you find the composition you prefer. I often use L-shapes cut out from picture mounts to choose which parts of an image I want to use. Here I have done this on several prints of the image, then I have cut out sections I might want to use.

2 Photocopy the image in sections, in colour, on ordinary paper and enlarge them to the size you need. I lightened this image and printed it out in three parts, top, middle and bottom. I then enlarged them by 50%, each to A4 size. Trim off any edges.

3 Stick the parts of the image together again using masking tape. Use soft pastels to alter the image to suit your purposes. Here I have removed a second tree to make a focal point of the main tree, and I have extended the field on the left to cover the extra tree and its shadow. I also added hills in the background to add interest to the scene.

4 Place a piece of tracing paper over your image and trace the main lines of the picture, first with an HB propelling pencil, then with a permanent marker.

5 Tape your tracing to a light box, then tape the fabric you will be using on top. Trace the image on to the fabric using an HB propelling pencil. Now you are ready to begin work on your stitched landscape.

Basic techniques

Here I show step by step how I construct my textile landscapes. The original photograph was taken on Lydney Park Estate, in Gloucestershire. The vivid yellow rapeseed field stood out against the green hills and the huge tree in the middle in contrasting dark green. The foreground field with the cut dried grass added greens, cream and beige, while a scattering of bright red poppies really added interest to the scene. When farmers started planting rapeseed, I did not like this acid yellow, but I have grown to love it as it stands out between the soft green fields and woods, making the landscape look like a patchwork quilt.

You will need

Shears, small sharp-pointed scissors and paper scissors

Pins, needles and thimble

Sewing machine with free machine embroidery foot and needles and 3 bobbins

Iron and baking parchment

Fusible web

Dark, medium, light and very pale blue organza, dyed cotton fabric, dyed yellow-green viscose, dyed yellow fine cotton, dyed green polyester/cotton, dyed scrim and muslin, dark brown dyed cotton, dyed dark green scrim, cotton backing fabric, cotton wadding (batting)

Pins, needle and thimble

Photocopy of the altered scene

HB pencil

Viscose machine embroidery threads

Tacking cotton

Quick unpick

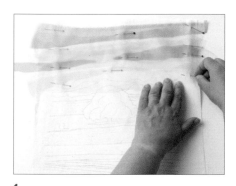

1 Lay strips of blue organza across the sky area, dark first, then paler, in random jagged strips. Pin them down as you go. Continue over the tops of the distant hills.

2 Cut out the hill shape from the photocopy of the altered scene and pin it to the dyed cotton hill fabric. Add a 5mm (¼in) seam allowance at the bottom and 2.5cm (1in) at the side edges. Cut out the shape.

3 Place the piece of fabric for the hills and pin it in place.

4 Cut out the shape of the distant tree line from the photocopy and use this as a pattern. Pin it to another brighter part of the same dyed fabric as the hills. Add a 5mm (¼in) seam allowance at the bottom and 2.5cm (1in) each side. Cut out, place and pin it on the landscape.

5 Cut a rectangle from dyed yellow-green viscose. I have doubled this over to achieve a depth of colour. Place and pin it going from the left of the image up to the tree in the middle. Repeat on the right.

6 Use the photocopy to make two patterns for the next line of trees, either side of the main tree. Place them on a lighter part of the dyed green fabric, leaving extra fabric at the sides and bottom. Pin in place.

Tip

You could simply layer the main tree on top of the background instead of leaving a space for it, but the landscape tends to get too thick, making stitching difficult.

7 Tear strips of yellow-dyed fine cotton for the rapeseed field. For the first row down, fold the top edge under and pin it. This is the turned edge appliqué technique.

8 Repeat on the right, leaving a space for the main tree. Use slightly stronger-coloured torn strips coming forwards and do not turn under the frayed edge this time, as it will create texture. Overlap the previous row.

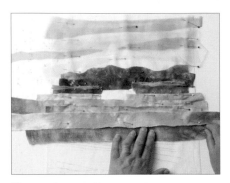

9 Add another torn strip of yellow-dyed fabric in front, then tear a strip of dull-green dyed muslin for the rape stems. Push this under the final row of rapeseed flowers and pin.

10 I have used a torn piece of green-dyed polyester/cotton for the foreground because although it does not dye well, polyester/cotton creates an interesting texture. Hold the piece in place so that you can see where to tear it off at the bottom. Snip the right-hand edge and tear across, then cut off the excess on the left.

11 The green polyester/cotton will suggest new grass coming through the dried, cut grass. For the dried grass, cut strips of dyed muslin and scrim. Place the strips at an angle in the field, trying different positions and not worrying if some pieces are twisted.

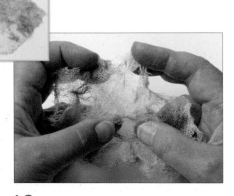

12 Cut an oval of dyed scrim and distress it by pulling the fibres apart to make thinner parts and holes. Pull out some of the threads. Place two pieces of distressed scrim in the foreground.

13 At this point, place the L shapes over the landscape to check how it is working as a composition. The frame should bring everything together and give you a chance to assess your progress so far.

  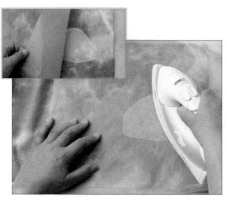

14 Turn the tracing over as you need the reverse of the tree shape. Trace the tree shape on to fusible web. Cut it out, leaving extra fusible web round the tree shape.

15 You need to choose a piece of dyed fabric for the tree shape that shows the light coming from the left. This will be the back of the fabric, so the lighter part should be on the right.

16 On your ironing board, layer baking parchment, the chosen area of fabric, fusible web, then more baking parchment to protect the iron, and iron the fusible web on to the fabric.

17 Cut out the tree shape, peel off the backing and place the tree on the landscape, taking out the pins from behind it. Pin the tree in place.

18 There is a gap in the rapeseed under the tree. Tear a strip of dark brown fabric and bend it into a curve. Take a pin out of a rapeseed strip and slip the cigar shape under it, and under the tree trunk. Pin it in place.

19 Layer baking parchment under and over the picture as in step 16 and press the tree shape on to the landscape. This technique is called fusible web appliqué. Distress a piece of dark green scrim and place two shapes, cut freehand, to suggest the shadowed side of the tree. Pin in place.

20 Use viscose machine embroidery thread to hand stitch down all the loose edges of the design. Remove the pins as you go. Use long stitches on the back but tiny stitches on the front so that they will not show, and use colours to match the fabrics.

Tip
Where pieces of fabric overlap each other, you only need to stitch the free edge.

21 The scrim in the foreground does not overlap, so you need to stitch along both top and bottom edges.

22 Layer from bottom to top: cotton backing fabric, cotton wadding cut slightly larger, and the landscape.

23 Pin the layers together in the middle first, then in the four corners. Use tacking cotton as this grips well. Cut a long piece and make a large knot in the end. Start with the knot on top in the middle of the top edge of the piece, and make large tacking stitches from the top to the bottom of the piece.

24 Tack a grid over the piece, using a new thread each time, going three times from top to bottom (with one row either side of the first row). Then start in the middle of one side and tack across from side to side in the same way. Add four more rows from side to side, making a total of five.

25 Choose thread colours for the sky. The idea is to blend two side-by-side fabric colours by choosing a thread that is between the two, to eliminate hard lines in the sky. Set up the sewing machine for free machine embroidery, with a grey thread in the bobbin, and the darkest blue as the top thread. Lower or cover the dogteeth, attach the free machine embroidery foot, loosen the top tension by one position, set the machine to straight stitch and move the stitch length to 0. Do a bit of practice stitching to make sure everything is working. Start in the middle of the top of the sky, pull the bobbin thread up to the top by winding by hand, put the foot down, and snip and pull out the end of the tacking. Begin stitching, moving the fabric from side to side and zigzagging unevenly from side to side in a fairly narrow band, going down the darkest strip of organza and a third of the way down the lighter strip. If the thread breaks, restart a couple of stitches back and rejoin.

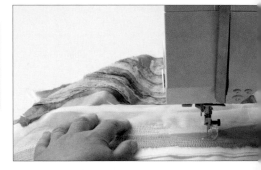

26 Move to the right and do another band of stitching in the same way, going between the edges of the previous band. Then move to the right again and repeat, continuing in this way out to the far right of the sky. To move to the left, turn the piece upside down to avoid crushing the landscape under the machine. Always choose the most comfortable and practical way of working. Continue making bands of stitching to blend the sky colours together. Remove the tacking stitches as you go.

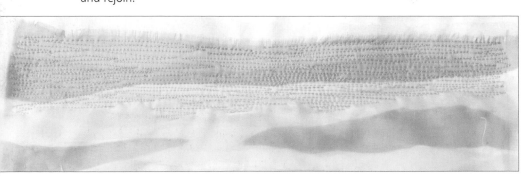

The top two bands of the sky, blended together with free machine embroidery stitching.

27 Change to the next lightest blue thread, as you will be working on the lighter strip of organza, and continue stitching from side to side, further down the sky this time. Overlap the previous, darker stitching to blend the colours.

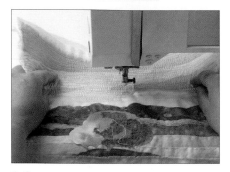

28 Once again, go right across the sky in this way, then continue downwards using the same colour, over the two darker strips of organza. Change to the light blue thread and continue.

29 Towards the bottom of the sky, use the lightest blue, and then change to white. As you stitch the very lowest part of the sky, you will need to hold back the fabric of the hills with a quick unpick.

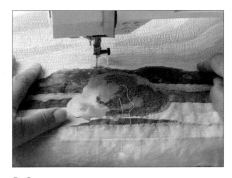

30 Stitch over the tops of the distant hills in the same way, using a medium grey-blue and following the contours of the hills. Go over each bit of stitching several times to reinforce the raw edge of the fabric.

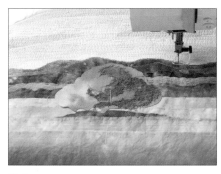

31 Stitch an outline to separate the distant hills from the slightly nearer hills. Follow the contours of the hills.

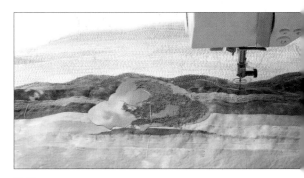

32 Change the top colour to medium lilac purple to create the mid-tones of the hills. Stitch more of this colour on to the sides of the hills facing the sun, and on the nearer hills.

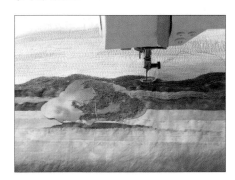

33 Change to medium navy blue and stitch the shadowed parts of the hills, following their contours, still in straight stitch, in bands that are not too wide.

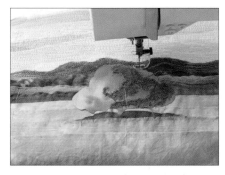

34 Stitch the darker parts of the hills with a dark blue-green thread, in the same way.

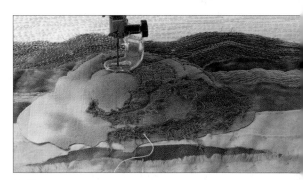

35 Use the same dark blue-green thread to outline the top of the tree, to anchor it. Also outline some of the areas within the tree, as shown.

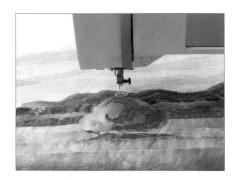

36 Use a dark charcoal grey to stitch the darkest hill shadows and a very pale lilac for the highlights.

37 Stitch the tree in dark, medium and light greens, following the circular shapes within the tree: work shadow on the right, medium tone in the centre and the lightest to the left of each shape. Highlight the edges of each shape with a few stitches in white. Use greens and grey to stitch the trunk, again using light tones on the left and shadow on the right.

38 Return to the background, and working from the centre tree outwards, stitch across the bottom of the hills to represent the trees in the distance. Start with the dark green thread, and machine in a circular movement, working the right-hand side of each tree and keeping the top edge irregular. Thread the machine with a medium green and stitch the middle section of each tree, then with the lightest green, highlight the left-hand side of each tree. To work the background fields, use thread matching the field and machine stitch straight lines from the centre tree outwards. Repeat on the opposite side. To work the cross-section hedges, take a medium green thread and stitch in guidelines. Continue in an irregular circular movement to create the hedge shape. Use dark thread and light green for shadows and highlights. For the nearest hedge, work in the same way as for the cross section hedges. Since this one is nearer, it will appear larger and will need more detail. Follow the general rules for shadow on the right, light on the left.

39 Stitch the main rapeseed field using a matching yellow thread. Start from the right-hand side of the main centre tree, working outwards a section at a time. Stop stitching when level with the bottom of the tree. Move to the left-hand side of the tree and repeat the sequence, starting at the top of the field. Stop when you are level with the bottom of the tree. For the tree shadow (an unplanted area), stitch two rows of yellow stitching under the tree branches. Machine stitch the shadowed, unplanted area with a few straight lines of brown thread, then with the green at the outside edges, with a few short lines, making an irregular shape. Continue with the yellow thread, working the rest of the field from the centre outwards as before. Work a few stitches into the shadowed area to show where a few flower seeds have grown, giving an uneven appearance. Continue stitching down to the green line of the fabric, constantly working from the centre outwards, staggering stitching as you go, as for the sky. Use light brown thread to stitch the lines made by the tractor, then use a few stitches in grey to emphasise some sections. For the front line (see the bottom of the picture), use a beige thread in a circular movement to get the effect of the shadow and to give depth to the flowers.

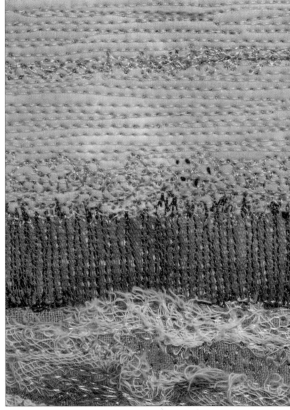

40 For the rapeseed stalks, from the centre use several different greens with a straight stitch, working up and down. At the top edge, stitch to uneven heights, as this will give a more natural look. For the bottom edge, use a darker green to emphasise the bottom of the stalks and the shadows. Use a darker shade of yellow to stitch along the top of the stalks randomly, to create the effect of individual flowers. With a circular movement, stitch one row along the top.

41 For the foreground field, thread the machine with a light beige thread and machine stitch scrim in place. Work from the middle outwards, adding extra scrim as you go if necessary. Work along the lines so that they look like cut dried grass. Stop and rethread the machine with green to stitch the new grass growing between the rows, in short up and down movements. Work a section at a time and do not be tempted to stitch all the lines of dried grass and then go back to stitch the newly grown grass, as this will cause uneven tension and distortion.

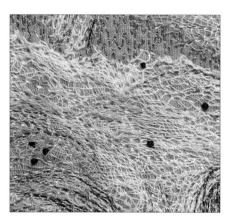

42 For the detail of the dried grasses, use grey, blue-grey, green and beige thread to emphasise the way the dried grass is laying. Stitch in the curves and layers. Finally use a dark grey for the shadows, and add highlights in white thread.

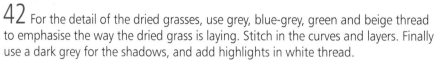

43 Stitch a few red French knots (see diagram) into the outer edge of the field. In the foreground where the dried grass is, stitch yellow French knots for the stray rapeseed flowers.

44 To finish, look over your work carefully. If there are areas which are raised, a little more stitching will normally flatten them. Finally, remember to sign your work. This can be your full name or your initials. I work my initials in machine stitching. Alternatively, you can sign on the back with a permanent acid-free marker pen.

Opposite
The finished piece.

Elements of the landscape

Skies

The sky is a very important element in any landscape picture. Dramatic sunsets and sunrises claim everyone's attention as the sun paints the sky with vivid reds, oranges and yellows. At other times the sky can be much more delicate, with pale pink, pale peach and turquoise – the most magical of sky colours. We are used to seeing blue skies on sunny days, and when you look and study them you will find all different shades of blue and white. Grey overcast skies can include blue-greys, pinkish greys, mauves, whites and yellowish greys. Stormy skies can be very dramatic, especially if there is thunder and lightning, including every colour from ink black to purple, navy blue and grey. The night sky in the moonlight is dark and dramatic with black, purples, grey and the silver from the moon.

Cloud formations can change as you watch depending on the strength of the wind in the atmosphere. Most people think clouds are white, grey and black, but look at the clouds and break down the colours present.

Not only does the sky show us roughly the time of day and the weather – it also adds colour, atmosphere and drama to any landscape picture.

This photograph was taken while on holiday in Yorkshire. This beautiful sunset sky had a huge range of colours including shades of orange, yellow, blue and grey. To enable you to identify the colours, try this exercise: paint a colour chart, using a separate square for each colour. You will be amazed how many colours and shades you can identify, and this will help you to replicate a complicated colour scheme.

Detail from the Waterfall picture on page 116. This shows a stormy day in Scotland; the sky is very dark blue, almost black. Storm clouds are rolling in towards the distant mountains and at the edge of the storm, the clouds are grey. You can still see the blue and white summer sky in the distance. The heavy clouds cast shadows on to the land, and the mountain in the distance is very dark as the sun is blocked out. The sky is made from space-dyed blue and white cotton overlaid with deep blue and navy organza, and the grey clouds are made from very fine distressed black chiffon. The sky has an amazing number of colours if you look closely: lots of different blues, navy, turquoise, mauves, greys and white, which I have emphasised by stitching with matching thread.

A stormy Scottish sunset with lots of different blues, mauves and greys. Look at the painting exercise and make your own paint chart when you have chosen your own design photograph. This will help you to decide which fabrics you need to produce your picture.

Sky detail from the Lavender Farm project on page 124: a beautiful pale blue summer sky with white fluffy clouds. I used pale blue and white space-dyed cotton, overlaying the white areas with a double layer of white crystal organza with fusible web appliqué. The blue parts of the sky were stitched with horizontal straight stitching and the white clouds were stitched in white thread worked in scalloped shapes to give the clouds a fluffy effect. The clouds were finally outlined in blue to emphasise their shapes.

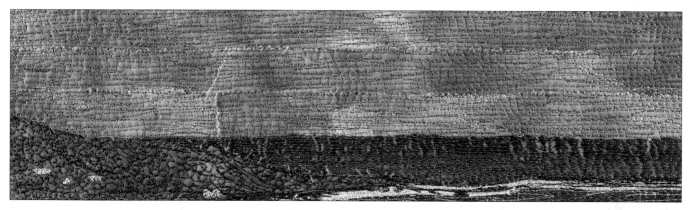

Detail from the Barbados picture One Moment in Time, page 7. I made the sky with the torn strip method (see page 32). Bright blue space-dyed cotton was heavily machine stitched with horizontal lines in blue and white. The photographic lights have picked up the joins in the strips so that you can see how pieces of fabric can be joined to get the effect you want.

Sky detail from the Poppy Fields piece on page 71. I used space-dyed pale blue and mainly white cotton to create lots of fluffy white clouds. I stitched the sky, changing from blue to white as required, using one of my favourite techniques that I have used for many years, a continuous swirl pattern stitched freehand to give a softer effect.

The sky from the Flower Garden project on page 95. For this sky I used a continuous swirl pattern, which I often use on my textile pictures and quilts. I find it gives interest as well as texture to a large flat area, blending all the different shades of blue together. This shows a beautiful summer's day with a vivid blue sky and only little wisps of white cloud. I used blue space-dyed cotton with tiny areas of very pale blue, which look like almost transparent wispy clouds.

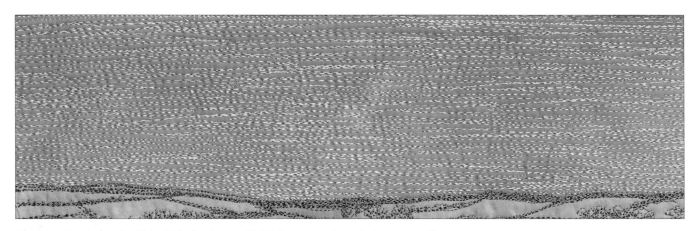

A leaden, wintry sky from the Winter Fields piece on page 75. This is an extremely simple sky using grey-blue cotton, heavily machine stitched with viscose thread.

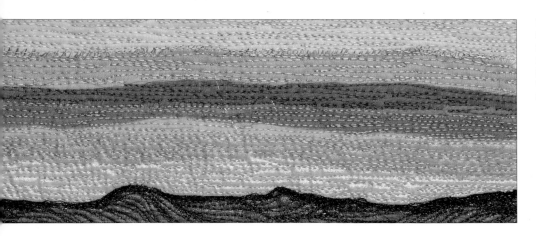

This is a very simple sunset. It is made from white cotton fabric overlaid with uneven torn strips of organza in blue, peach, orange, lilac, pink and metallic peach. When the organzas overlap, you get secondary colours. Machine stitching with matching viscose thread, working side to side with straight stitch, blends the colours together.

Stitched Sunset

The amazing photograph that led to this piece was taken while we where on holiday in Yorkshire. It features vivid oranges and golden clouds, while at the top of the picture, night-time clouds are beginning to converge. The black hill and the silhouettes of the trees against the sky make a strong statement.

I used mainly space-dyed cotton for this picture, except for the golden clouds. The large dark cloud was made with a piece of space-dyed silk velvet left over from fabric I dyed for my wedding jacket. There are some organza and chiffon pieces laid on to the sky to give secondary colours, and I distressed them to create three-dimensional effects. I used very simple machine stitching, contour stitching or random stitching, leaving the colourful fabrics to provide the illusion of this beautiful sky. The silhouetted trees are machine stitched with black viscose thread, giving lots of detail of their bare branches and shapes.

Water

Puddles, streams, rivers, lakes, ponds, waterfalls and canals can all be used to enhance a landscape. Water is a magical element in a landscape; it gives light, reflections, movement, colour, distance and drama. Water reflects the light from the sky and colour from the surrounding landscape. This can make the water look golden, green, blue, brown, grey or any number of vivid oranges and reds when there is a sunset or autumn trees.

Movement is also an element to consider when stitching textile landscapes, and if you include water, you can show the fast-flowing water of streams, rivers and waterfalls, which can be very dramatic, with white water splashing on to the rocks. Alternatively you might depict the stillness of lakes and ponds with plants such as waterliles and leaves floating on the water, or the mirror images of trees, buildings and bridges.

Detail from the Waterfall piece on page 116. The water travels from the top of the mountains to the rocks' edge, then falls from a great height into a rocky bowl where it collects before spilling over the edge from two separate places into two individual waterfalls. The waterfalls then cascade over the rocks, combining and separating as the water tumbles and twists down the mountainside.
I made the water with two layers of crystal organza, appliquéd with fusible web. I machine stitched it with white viscose thread, following the flow of the water, and a little silver metallic thread to add extra sparkle as the light hits the water.

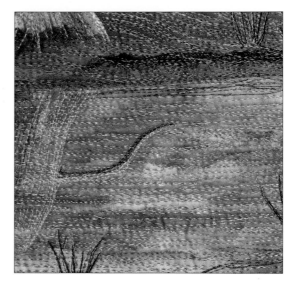

Water detail from the tree piece shown on pages 76–77. The reflection of the tree makes a mirror image in the water. The ripples from the moving water travel through the reflection, creating a transparent effect. Strips of space-dyed cotton have been used for the water, overlaid with green and blue shimmering organza to replicate the colourful reflection of the surrounding scenery.

This simple landscape was made for a teaching workshop, and was inspired by the wonderful Lake District. It introduces the elements required to achieve sky, hills, water and reflections on a beautiful summer's day. The sky is a hand-dyed cotton fabric overlaid with strips of blue organza: vivid blue at the highest point receding to pale blue behind the hills. The stitching lines on the hills identify their undulating contours or ruggedness The water is very still with the reflection of the hills and sky in the lake created by overlaying different coloured organza. In the distance at the water's edge there is a line of reflected light, which gives life, depth and interest to the picture.

Detail from One Moment in Time on page 7. A Caribbean summer's day on the beautiful island of Barbados. The water is a collection of amazing colours: vivid blues, greens, turquoise and mauves. It was created with organza strips in these colours, over a base of blue space-dyed fabric and the sparkle of a few metallic fabric strips. To give distance in the water, there is more detail in the foreground, emphasised with white and silver stitching for the crests of the waves.

Sunset

This piece was done for a simple teaching workshop, using lots of different coloured organza. The technique I have used shows how to overlay the main sunset-coloured organza to portray the sky and the reflection in the water. This method will also give you lots of wonderful secondary colour where the organza pieces overlap. The tops of the mountains are touched by the sunset colours, so I have used peach and orange colours there too. The reflection of the mountains in the water takes on a purple appearance against the fiery sunset reflection. The piece was heavily machine quilted and embroidered with viscose thread. It makes an ideal colourful first attempt at this technique.

Detail from the Cannop Ponds piece page 73, showing the reflections from the background trees and reeds. The reflections colour the water with beautiful purples, browns, pinks and oranges. I have used space-dyed cotton, organza and viscose machine embroidery thread to give the shimmer.

Detail of the foreground reeds standing in the water. The water shines and glistens between the reeds, with lots of colours reflected in the water from the surrounding trees and reeds. The technique used was overlaying organza on to the base fabric, plus lots of coloured viscose thread.

Detail showing the reflection of the reeds standing in the water. I have portrayed the water rings around the base of the stems and the zigzags created when the straight stems are reflected in the moving water. I used a straight machine stitch for this, working from side to side in a zigzag movement with a dark green viscose thread.

Detail from the Anticipation piece shown on page 97. In a Barbados garden, a pelican stands on the pebbled edge of a dark mysterious pond. Shaded by trees and flowers, the water is a deep, dark blue, and even though the pond is in shadow, the lower edge of the pebble bank and the bottom of the pond are still visible through the beautifully clear water. The pond base is made from space-dyed pink, blue and grey cotton; the same fabric as the garden background. This is overlaid with blue, dark green, dark purple, black and navy space-dyed silk chiffon, distressed to give the shadow effect, with white viscose stitching for light reflection.

For this piece I space dyed a large piece of fine cotton fabric, using shades of turquoise, lilac, blue and a tiny amount of yellow. The end product was fantastic – a wonderful water fabric. No additional enhancement was required to achieve the movement and colour of the water. I needed to keep the design simple, leaving the fabric to shine through in all its glory, and I decided an abstract design was required. I used all the fabric as I made a long picture which I love, as well as four cushion covers which could later be framed as pictures in their own right. Each of the pieces is cut and stitched in a slightly different way. I cut this piece of fabric into a wave shape. A strip of soft washed calico was cut in the same wave shape to fit in between the two pieces of water fabric, and a second piece of calico was cut with the top edge in the wave shape and the bottom edge straight. I stitched both pieces in place and pressed them, then mounted them on to wadding and backing cotton. I machine quilted through all thicknesses. For the middle section, I stitched contour lines following the wave design line. The top and bottom sections also have contoured stitching, but for these the stitching has a more rippling effect. I have two knitting yarns: a bouclé with white and different coloured blue knobbly pieces to emphasise some of the lines, and another with a fringe that was too long, so I trimmed it to the length I wanted. Both yarns were couched in place using a small zigzag machine stitch, but they could be couched by hand.

47

Trees & woodlands

There are an amazing number of different tree species throughout the world from giant trees like the kauri and redwoods to the small, twisted trees of very dry, arid lands. I really enjoy stitching trees into landscape pictures, as they add interest, distance and colour to every scene. One tree on its own will make a statement. Several trees will create lots of interest, while trees in a woodland standing majestically together can make a beautiful landscape picture. Whether trees are vibrant with autumn leaves, misshapen with growths or missing limbs, falling down or even dead, they are all interesting to draw, photograph and stitch. Deciduous trees take on a totally different outline in the winter, when they become very sculptural with skeletal branches reaching for the sky.

Tree trunks are often incorrectly described as brown, but they are many colours including grey, purple, pink, white and even black on rainy days. They often have fungus, lichens, ivy and moss growing on them, which can change their appearance to shades of orange, green and silver. Look at the texture and patterns of the trunks, from the peeling bark of the silver birch to the rough patterning of oak trees.

Every aspect of a tree's life creates beauty, from the first growth until it dies, eventually rotting to becomes home to many insects and fungi.

Opposite
Bluebell Picture

This picture was worked on one piece of green space-dyed cotton. The background trees were machine stitched without detail or definition, to give them a hazy, distant look. The bluebells were made from torn strips of blue, mauve and green space-dyed cotton with short brown strips for the path showing through. I machine stitched in straight stitch horizontally from side to side to blend all the fabrics together. Detail on the tree trunks was worked with space-dyed scrim to create the bark texture, with green scrim for the moss. The light on the left-hand sides of the trunks was portrayed with pale green scrim, highlighted with white stitching. Mauve and purple scrim were used to show the shadows, and dark purple chiffon and viscose fabric for the cast shadow on the ground and on the right-hand sides of the trees. I gathered and distressed green chiffon for the branches and leaves, free machine stitching using circular and oval movements to represent the leaves.

Below: three different types of autumn foliage from the Cannop Ponds piece on page 73.

This section shows larch trees taking on the creams and golds of autumn. Interlaced with them are the purple branches of silver birches, having lost their leaves. The base fabrics were space-dyed cottons in the colour of the trees, appliquéd in place. They were then heavily machine stitched with viscose thread to show the detail.

The leaves of the huge oak trees have changed to wonderful oranges, reds and gold. Across the middle and the bottom right-hand corner, silver birches, having lost their leaves, take on a mauve hue. To the right there is a line of creamy larch trees.

This detail shows a huge oak tree on the left. The very dense foliage has changed to autumn tints: deep oranges and reds with purple shadows. The right-hand tree is a silver birch with the light catching the skeletal branches, changing the purple to pale mauve. In the bottom right-hand corner there are bushes which are still green. I appliquéd small pieces of fabric for the trees, then heavily machine stitched to enhance the colours and show the shapes of the trees and individual branches.

Middle distance trees from the Winter Fields piece on page 75. The hedgerow at the bottom of the field has some trees still growing to their full height. The hedge and the trees were created with dark green space-dyed cotton. I then stitched both the trees and the hedge with dark green thread, extending beyond the fabric to show the bare branches.

This detail of the bluebell wood in the Memories of Happy Days picture on pages 86–87 shows the sun shining through the trees, lighting up the left-hand side of all the trunks as well as the background. There are areas of bright white sunlight on the ground, taking the colour from the bluebells, with much deeper vibrant colours in the shade of the trees and very dark cast shadows to the right of the tree trunks.

A detail of the main tree trunk from same bluebell picture on pages 86–87. This shows how the very versatile space-dyed scrim fabric can give texture and colour. The left-hand side of the trunk has very pale green frayed scrim; the bottom middle has green scrim to show where the moss is growing; and there are greys and mauves, then purples on the shadowed side.

This detail from the piece on pages 76–77 shows how the distant trees are created using a much simpler technique. Space-dyed green cotton and straight stitching were used to outline the dome shapes of the leaf-covered branches. This technique complements the detail of the foreground trees.

50

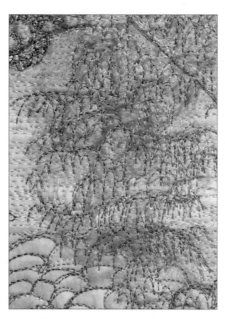

Detail from pages 76–77 showing an old oak tree. I created the effect of the leaves using layers of green chiffon, which I distressed by gathering and making small holes. I then used green viscose thread for heavy stitching in random, circular free machine embroidery movements.

Foliage detail from the same picture. Silver birch trees have delicate foliage that hangs downwards on thin twigs. To achieve this effect I have again used green chiffon but this time a single layer and only slightly distressed. I used free machine embroidery with green viscose thread in straight lines to give that delicate effect.

A detail from the oak tree trunk on the left of the picture. It is lit on the right and shadowed on the left. The tree is leaning to the left, so there is a greater area of light on the tree trunk. I have used fine chiffon in different shades to show the shadows and middle section shading, with a lot of free machining to give the shape.

A further detail from the same picture. Silver birch tree trunks are very distinctive, with white bark and dark markings around the trunk where the bark has started to peel. The details on the trunks were stitched with free machine embroidery.

A tree trunk reflected in the water. To create reflections like this, take your tree pattern and turn it down over the water section to ensure you get the correct angle and create a mirror image. Notice you do not see the base of the tree trunk because the tree is above and away from the water's edge. Always check your original photograph or drawing to ensure you have the reflection correct.

Hills & mountains

What is the difference between a mountain and a hill? I think of hills as having a soft, rolling outline, while mountains are huge, craggy and rocky, finishing with a peak or summit. Hills and mountains take on different colours; in the distance they can become very pale green, grey, blue or purple, but if the mountain has bare rock, or is covered with snow, it can reflect the colour of a sunset, showing bright pinks and oranges. Shown here are a selection of hills and mountains created in fabric and stitching, in lots of different shades and colours. Study hills and mountains and see how they constantly change in colour and tone due to weather, time of day and distance.

Gentle rolling hills of an English countryside. These were very simply worked, with the hills in different shades of appliquéd green space-dyed cotton and the furthest hill in a darker shade to show shadow. The machine stitching emphasises the contours and gentle slopes, giving lots of shape to the hills.

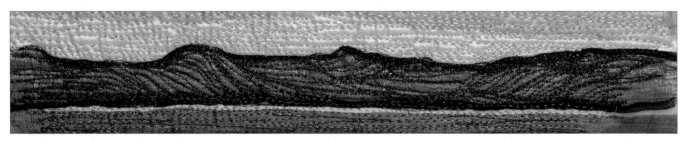

Distant mountains at sunset; a detail from the Sunset piece on page 46. The evening light has tinted the tops of the mountains, which have taken on the oranges and peaches of the setting sun. The lower edge of the peach organza is overlapped with the edge of a torn strip of semi-transparent dark aubergine viscose. This was machine stitched in matching viscose thread to show the contours of the mountains.

Detail from One Moment in Time, page 7. This Barbados landscape shows many hills rolling down to the sea. It was made from torn strips of space-dyed cotton, giving lots of different subtle colours which add interest to the hills. I heavily machine stitched the hills to identify different coloured areas and vegetation.

Detail from Through the Valley, pages 106 and 107. This shows Lake District hills and mountains, with shades of green used for the hills and purples for the mountains. The tops of the mountains were constructed with turned edge appliqué in which the edges are folded under (see step 7, page 32), and the foreground with torn strip appliqué (see page 32), all in space-dyed cotton. Machine stitching was used to emphasise the contours of the mountains and hills. As the mountains recede into the distance, they get paler, showing less detail.

Detail from the Waterfall piece on page 116. Storm clouds are gathering over the mountains, giving them a darker coloration; the far distant mountain is very dark. Torn strip appliqué (see page 32), with green cotton overlaid with space-dyed distressed scrim was used at the top and on both sides of the foreground mountain. I used grey space-dyed cotton for the area with the waterfall, which shows the bare dark-grey rock formation. Heavy machine stitching was used to show all the details.

A strange yellow and blue stormy sky gives this picture a dark, heavy look. The mountains are made with torn strips of purple, blue and green space-dyed cotton, and the hillside with a mixture of autumnal colours. The sunlight is coming through the clouds and is lighting up the lower hillside, field and trees, which were all made with torn strip appliqué (see page 32).

Flowers in the landscape

Wild and cultivated flowers make a wonderful, colourful addition to any landscape, whether you portray an accent flower, a field, garden or a woodland full of flowers. Deciding how to portray the flowers will depend on how far away they are and how much detail you wish to show. Colour and shape are the most important elements. If the flowers are en masse in the distance, such as poppies, bluebells or rapeseed, blocks of the relevant colour will identify the flower species, because you will know which flowers to expect in a field or woodland situation. When flowers are closer to you in the foreground, you need to show more detail, and this is when the shape becomes more important. Poppy heads take on a flat circular shape as they get closer, (see the foreground flowers in the Poppy Fields piece on page 71). When really close, the petals take shape and you can see the detail of the black centres, which can perhaps be enhanced with tiny black beads. Rapeseed flowers can be shown with clusters of French knots. Bluebells have arched stems with many bell-shaped flowers on each stem. Fabric can be cut in the flower shape and appliquéd into place by hand or machine for foreground flowers, and extra detail can be hand or machine embroidered. If you iron fusible web on to the fabric before cutting it out, then cut very small pieces, you will be able to achieve minute detail and attach each individual petal before stitching.

This is a demonstration piece, working flowers with hand embroidery, using just French knots, plus variations of this stitch. Pieces of ruched chiffon are laid under the stitching to give depth of colour.

Different sizes of French knots are made by using one, two, three or more strands of six-strand embroidery cotton, combined before stitching. You could also use other embroidery threads such as cotton perle or tapestry wool. The stitch variations are:

Long-legged French knots. Instead of taking the needle back down into the fabric at the making of the knot, take the needle down away from the knot, making a leg or tail.

Bullion knots. Twist the thread around the needle until you have the length of knot required. Lay the stitch on to the fabric and take the needle back down through the fabric at the end of the bullion knot.

Looped bullion knots. Twist the thread around the needle to make a bullion knot but instead of laying it flat, take the needle back into the same place, which means the knot curls up into a loop.

Bullion knot tightened at the one end to give a narrowing of the stitch by pulling the twist tight.

Garden landscape

This piece features French knots, single fly stitch, straight stitch and satin stitch. It was worked on painted habatoi silk, mounted on cotton fabric with small pieces of ruched chiffon under the stitching to give depth of colour. It was stitched in an embroidery hoop.

Background foliage: single fly stitch and straight stitch.

Tree blossom: French knots worked with one, two or three strands of cotton embroidery thread to create different size blossoms.

Tulips: worked with satin stitch.

Daffodils: worked in French knots because they are in the background and do not have much detail.

Muscari or grape hyacinth: tiny French knots in three shades of blue: light, medium and dark.

Aubretia: tiny single-strand French knots in purple and blue.

Alyssum: single-strand French knots in golden yellow.

Lace Lavender Fields

This landscape is a very simple interpretation of the Snows Hill lavender fields, in the Cotswolds, which I designed for a workshop. The picture is made from space-dyed cotton lace, scrim and fine cotton fabric. I have used a bright, summery blue space-dyed cotton for the sky. I used two different shades of purple dye for the lavender, to give variation in the colour, and different strengths of dye to give light and shade. Some of the lace, cotton and scrim were dyed with a dark green and a light green dye for the grass, the lavender stems and the trees on the horizon, again using different strengths of dye for variety. The cotton lace worked in straight lines for the lavender proved very effective. See page 118 for a project that shows an alternative technique for the lavender fields, leading to a more detailed picture.

Detail from the Peace and Tranquillity piece on page 96. Each water lily flower was made from pink space-dyed cotton fabric. I placed the flower pattern on the fabric, choosing an area with a lighter coloured section on the left-hand side of the flower. All details of the petals were machine embroidered with viscose machine embroidery thread: dark pink and purple for the shadows and medium and pale pink for the lighter side, with white for the highlights. The lily pads were cut from green space-dyed cotton fabric. Again, I chose sections from my dyed fabric carefully to get the light and shade and to show a dappled effect from the surrounding trees. The leaves were stitched from the centre radiating outwards with a darker green thread then machine stitched around the leaf edge several times.

Foreground detail from the Poppy Fields piece on page 71. This was made from one piece of red space-dyed cotton which had lovely markings from the dye, so I decided to let the fabric lead my stitching, and as a result the detail became slightly abstract. For the large poppy heads, I stitched around some of the bright red areas in circles, for the others I cut small circles of bright red viscose fabric and appliquéd them in place by machining around the circles. Machining with dark green thread, I followed some of the dye markings to create lovely shapes for the stems. The white petals of the moon daisies were machined, with yellow French knots for the centres. I hand stitched clusters of yellow French knots for a few remaining rapeseed flowers. I then beaded the poppy centres with tiny black glass beads.

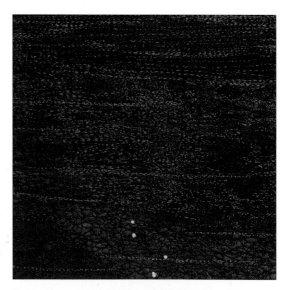

Middle distance detail of the same Poppy Fields piece. The poppies blend into a block of red as they recede into the distance. To make this, I overlaid the remaining field with red organza, which gave a more even colour. I stitched some lines of green for shadow and some green from the flowerless rapeseed plants. I hand stitched yellow French knots for isolated rape flowers. The whole of the poppy field is free machine embroidered.

Detail from Anticipation, page 97. This section shows the bougainvillea climbing plant and the large banana plant leaves.

I backed some green space-dyed cotton with fusible web and cut out lots of little pointed leaves, some from light areas and others from dark areas. I made the bracts with magenta space-dyed habotai silk. I backed the silk with fusible web and cut out small clusters of pointed bracts. I positioned the leaves and bracts on the background fabric and pressed them in place with a warm iron, making sure I covered them first with baking parchment to prevent the silk from melting. I machine stitched round the outside of the leaves and added detail to the bracts, separating them into individual petal shapes with stitching. The banana plant leaves were also cut from fusible web-backed green space-dyed cotton, with care taken to choose light and dark parts of the fabric, then machined in place.

Bluebell carpet detail from Memories of Happy Days, pages 86–87. When millions of bluebells grow together in the distance, they become a blur or block of different shades of blue. As they tend to grow under trees in a woodland situation, they are often interspersed with dark purple shadows from the trees and light areas where the sunlight streams through the branches, making a patchwork of different shades and blue tones. This bluebell carpet was created with torn strips of blue, mauve, and purple space-dyed cotton, with small pieces of bright green fabric for shoots of new grass, and brown for the pathway.

57

Distance

In order to create convincing distance in your textile landscapes, study your source photograph, looking carefully at how the landscape recedes into the distance. The colours usually become paler and cooler, the trees, hedges and buildings get smaller and details become less obvious. You can interpret the distance in the source picture by paying attention to these details of perspective, colour warmth and tone.

Detail from Winter Fields on page 75, showing the trees in the middle distance. There are still some details; you can see the shape of each tree, as well as light and shade on the branches. The distant hills take on a blue haze, very pale in colour. All the hedges and trees are grey-blue with no detail, only height and shape to suggest the difference between trees and hedges. The middle trees were created with appliquéd space-dyed fabric with machine-stitched details. In the far distance, the hedges and trees are machine stitched in a pale blue-grey thread.

Detail from the Waterfall piece, page 116. This piece relies on the perspective of the waterfall seen flowing from the mountain top down into the foreground. The distant mountain top looks dark because of the gathering storm clouds blocking out the sun. The top of the cliff is very bright as the sun shines through a gap in the storm clouds. The size of the background mountain shows that it is a long way in the distance. This mountain was created using fusible web appliqué.

Detail from the Poppy Fields piece on page 71. May Hill is in the background. Because it is in the far distance, it has taken on a blue haze. Machine stitching was used to create the illusion of hedges and fields in blue-grey thread. As the land gets closer, you begin to see some detail: a little white stitching gives the illusion of houses, circular stitching is used to look like trees, and light green stitching shows where the sun lights up the land. The middle distance shows the trees with lots of detail; you can see the rounded shapes of the trees and the light and shade of each branch, giving a three-dimensional effect. The sun lights up the larger, brighter fields as they come forwards, until they disappear from view into the valley with the edge of the poppy field just coming into view.

This detail of the same piece shows the far distance where you can see May Hill, which looks quite blue with very little detail; there is only a hint of the hedges and the fields. Blue-grey machine stitching was used for the trees and hedges, with little bits of yellow-green stitching to highlight where the sun just catches the fields. Lower down, dark green stitching in small circles was used to represent the trees. Little specks of white stitching are sufficient to show the houses. The famous trees on top of May Hill are represented by machine stitching in blue-grey thread, worked in small dense circles to show that there are many trees. There are said to be ninety-nine.

Detail from One Moment in Time on page 7. As the sky meets the deep blue of the sea in this Barbados landscape, there is a thin imaginary line. Even though there is no detail it is obvious because of the depth of colour that the sea goes out a considerable distance before meeting the horizon. On the land the only detail is provided by a few white stitching lines, creating the illusion of white buildings among the trees, suggested by dark green stitching in a circular motion. The spit of land reaching out into the sea is mainly visible because of the white sand, stitched with pale beige thread. The water in the bay changes colour as the light catches it, turning it to different shades of blue, green and purple. I used torn strips of organza in different colours, laid over the space-dyed blue cotton to replicate these wonderful colours, then machined then in place.

Foregrounds

A textile picture is largely two-dimensional so we need to create the illusion of distance, making it look like a three-dimensional scene. We do this by creating foreground, middle ground and background areas. The plants and trees in the foreground will be larger, with lots of detail, and the colours at the front will be stronger than in the rest of the picture (see the poppy detail picture below). As plants and trees recede into the distance, they become smaller, and if you look at the lavender field detail below, you can see that the rows of lavender become narrower, following the rules of linear perspective (see page 18).

Detail from the Poppy Fields piece on page 71. The poppies in the foreground are large enough to show the black centres, which I have beaded to give more detail. You can see the individual white petals and the yellow centres of the moon daisies, and small yellow French knots represent the few rapeseed flowers that are still blooming.

Detail from the Lavender Farm project shown in full on page 124. The lavender flowers are larger nearer to the front of the picture. The tall cream grasses stand out against the lavender. You can see each individual green grass tuft with details of light and shade. The lavender rows get narrower and the flowers less distinct as the scene recedes.

Detail from the summer section of the Forest of Dean quilt, shown on page 70. The foxgloves stand tall in the foreground of the picture – they can grow to 2.1m (7t) tall. The leaves were appliquéd with fusible web, and the flowers were stitched with six different pinks, plus white to create the shape and lots of detail.

Detail from the foreground of the Through the Valley piece shown on pages 106–107. In this picture you can see how the colour pales as you travel back into the picture. The grass tufts are larger in the foreground and there is more detail in and around the water.

Foreground detail from the bluebell panel, part of the Misty and Music quilt. Near the front of the picture you can see how the dainty bluebells curve over, making the little flowers hang down. You can see at the top of this section behind the legs of the deer where the bluebells are becoming just a haze of blue.

Fields & grasses

Fields feature in many landscapes, and can be planted with arable crops, such as corn, wheat, and rapeseed, or with grass that has been closely cropped by grazing animals. Fields in the landscape can show distance, perspective and the contours of the land. Grasses come in many species from ornamental brightly coloured grasses for the garden to reeds at the water's edge and the coarse grass which animals cannot eat, standing tall on marshes and moor lands. Grass can grow tall against buildings, fences and other inaccessible places where it cannot be cut or grazed, and can become dry and old, turning cream in colour as it dies. Grass in the foreground can help to create perspective and scale in the landscape.

A piece depicting tall ornamental garden grass plants in greens and oranges, showing different heights, and how the grass bends, creating a more natural look. This was hand embroidered with six-strand embroidery thread using only one strand at a time.

Detail from the bottom right-hand side of the New Forest picture shown on pages 76 and 77. The foreground short grass is trimmed by the wild ponies, and I made it from torn strips of green space-dyed cotton. The clumps of tall, tough, reed-like grasses were stitched on the machine with light and dark brown threads to show the light and shade. I stitched the reeds at different angles so that they look natural as if they are bending and moving in the breeze.

Detail from the Cannop Ponds piece on page 73. A dense area of reeds grow at the water's edge around the ponds. I stitched the very tall reeds in the nearest foreground, showing them bending over the water. I used dark green, brown and orange for the light and shadow on the stems and leaves.

Detail from the Winter Fields piece on page 75. The front field has the cut corn stalks showing through the snow. I stitched the stalks by hand using only one strand of six-strand embroidery thread. I worked straight stitches, making the stalks shorter and the rows narrower as they go into the distance, and stitched some of the stalks at angles or bent them to make them look more natural. The fields slope into the valley from both sides. The second field has the light reflecting on to the snow because of the angle, so it is very white. As the fields recede into the distance, they gradually take on a bluish shade.

Detail from The Old Wood Shed on page 125. Around the shed, tall grasses have grown, and as they never get cut, they have dried and turned a cream colour. There are also some beside the tubs. By the shed doorway and in the background you can see more grass and some brown bracken and to the left, overgrowing the shed door, there are arching and trailing bramble stems.

Rocks & pebbles

To depict realistic rocks and pebbles you need to create the illusion of solid shapes, which can be achieved by adding shadows. I have either used a darker fabric for the shadow area, or machine stitching in a darker thread. For small pebbles, you can stitch around a the area several times to pull in the fabric, causing the wadding and the fabric to puff up, or you can stitch the underside with a darker thread, or both.

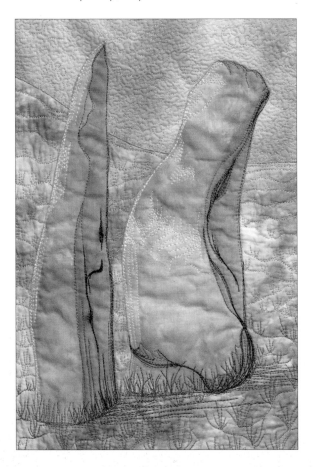

Detail from my Misty and Music quilt, showing two of the very tall modern standing stones recently erected at Lydney Docks on the banks of the River Severn. They were made from space-dyed beige cotton, and I used the darker areas of the fabric for the shadowed side of the stones. I used machine stitching in a darker thread to create the shapes of the stones and emphasise the sharp edges. I added highlights in white on the left-hand side where the light catches.

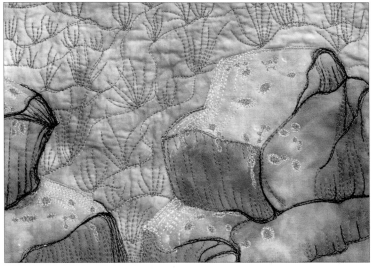

Rock detail from the standing stones panel of the Misty and Music quilt. These rocks are squarer in shape and grey in colour. I used the lighter and darker areas of grey space-dyed fabric to show the shape and shade. I emphasised the stones with machine stitching: white for highlights and darker thread for the shadows. I added delicate yellow and orange lichen circles.

Detail from the Anticipation piece on page 97. The bank of pebbles edging the pond is made from one piece of space-dyed stone-coloured cotton. Using the small areas of different shades of colour to distinguish each pebble, I machine stitched around the pebble shapes many times with a dark brown thread. I made the pebbles different sizes and shapes and created shadow at the bottom of each, using a machine straight stitch and curving each line slightly.

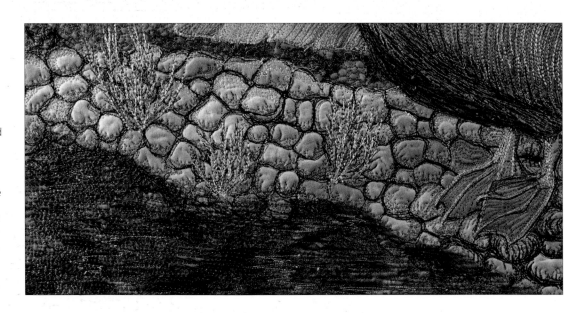

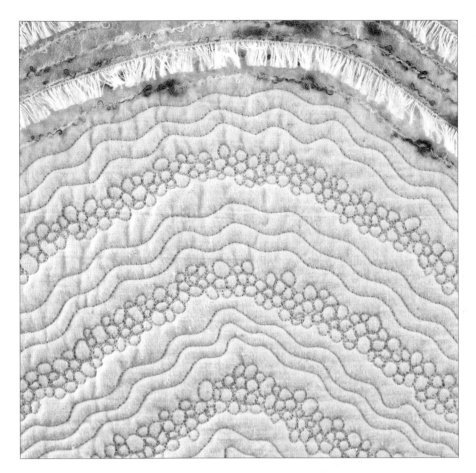

Detail from the large modern water piece on page 117. Stylized pebbles were stitched on a cream calico base fabric and the pebbles rely totally on the continuous machine stitching around each shape. When stitching pebbles, always make them different sizes and shapes. I stitched at least twice around each pebble to emphasise the shape, and this made them stand out as the stitching pulled each circle in, making the wadding and fabric puff up to give the illusion of pebbles.

Detail from the Waterfall piece on page 116. The rock section was made with grey space-dyed cotton fabric. Following the patterns in the dyed fabric and the photograph showing the rock formation, I stitched outlines with dark grey thread around each area to represent the rocks and pebbles. For the foreground rocks and pebbles, I machine stitched around each shape. If you find your fabric has an area which is not suitable, cut out a circle or oval shape from another area of the remaining space-dyed fabric, lay it in position and stitch around it to blend it in with the other rocks. I attached some space-dyed, distressed green scrim to look like moss growing on the rocks near the water's edge.

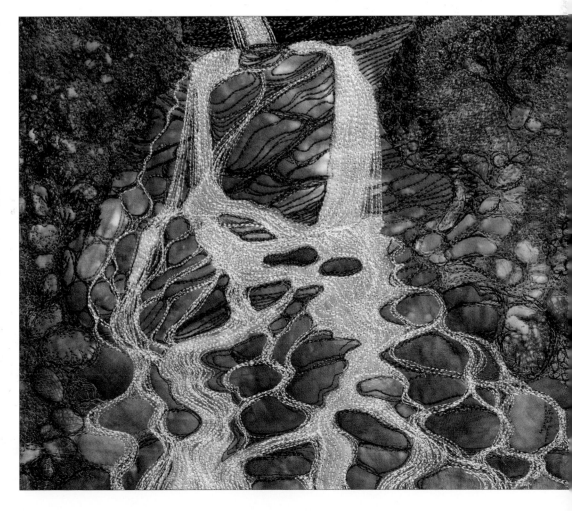

Buildings in the landscape

Buildings have a hard, solid structure, so to achieve this effect I usually appliqué the fabric with fusible web, which gives the stark, smooth outline to the walls and the roof (see the detail picture below). The basic shape of doors and windows can also be worked in this way. It adds realism to machine stitch details such as windows, roof tiles, guttering and doors. As buildings recede into the distance, they reduce in size. At a greater distance the whole building and the detail can be machine stitched, as in the Lavender Farm project on page 124 and the distant buildings on the right-hand side of the One Moment in Time picture on page 7.

Detail from the Naas House piece on pages 126–127. The house is very old and the walls are not completely straight, but using fusible web appliqué allows you to cut the fabric to exactly the right shape. I have used a space-dyed fabric, which was mainly white with pale shades of pink, and this has given the effect of old paint and light reflected on the building. I machine stitched detail on the roofs and the tower on top of the building. For the windows, I stitched the outline, then just the shadows as if light is bouncing off the glass. The guttering, chimneys and shadow on the left-hand side of the house were machine stitched in straight lines, with a few white lines added for highlights.

Detail of the barns from the Naas House piece. I used fusible web appliqué in space-dyed grey shaded cotton for the barns and rust-coloured cotton for the roofs. I then machine stitched the lines for the corrugated tin roofs. The windows and hay loft doors were outlined in machine stitching and then a few lines were added for details.

Detail from my Barbados landscape picture, One Moment in Time, on page 7, showing different-sized houses and huge villas among the trees. I used fusible web appliqué in white cotton fabric for the walls of the buildings with red roofs. The windows were stitched as simple filled-in squares. All you can see of the building in the foreground is the roof with just one white line for the walls, because it is hidden by the trees.

Detail from The Old Wood Shed on page 125. The sides of the old shed are made from planks of wood. I cut the side of the shed and the top of the doorway from one piece of pale blue-grey space-dyed cotton and appliquéd this with fusible web.
I used space-dyed scrim in greys, cut into strips, distressed and laid on to the shed side for texture. I machined these in place with pale greys and blues. The planks are outlined in dark grey to show each individual piece as well as its angle, and any splits in the wood. The shed roof is rust-coloured cotton, machine stitched in lines to suggest the tin sheets. The new shed in the background is made from grey-brown cotton for the wall and blue-grey cotton for the roof felt. Horizontal lines of machine stitching show the planks of the wall.

The seasons

Every season has a special look and the weather makes a great difference to the colours you will use in your stitched landscapes.

Spring

Bluebell Carpet

This is the spring section of my Forest of Dean quilt. The woodland is bathed in sunlight, streaming through the trees from the left. I used the torn strip technique (see page 32) for the bluebells, pathway and undergrowth. There are lots of appliqué trees, gradually reducing in size as they recede into the distance. I used distressed chiffon for the leaves. The background is one piece of dyed fabric with machine-embroidered tree trunks.

Opposite
Bluebells on the Malvern Hills, Worcestershire.

I first saw this amazing hill covered in bluebells in the spring of 1966. I was teaching at St James's Girls School, West Malvern, Worcestershire. The bluebell hill was so different from what I was used to at home, where the bluebells mainly grow under the trees in a woodland situation.

In 2009 I was asked to participate in an exhibition at the Weavers' Gallery in Ledbury, Herefordshire, commemorating the life and music of Sir Edward Elgar on the 75th anniversary of his death. The picture was inspired by part of a quote from Elgar: 'The trees are singing my music. Or have I sung theirs?' Elgar and his wife Alice are buried at St Wulstans Church, which stands on the other side of this beautiful hill in Malvern.

When you see the millions of bluebells, the colour is so intense that it is spellbinding. I have taken many photographs of this scene, and my favourite by far has this silver birch tree in the foreground. The silver and grey of the tree and the purple-blue of the bluebells create a magical combination.

I space-dyed my fabrics to achieve the vivid purple-blues of the bluebells and the many different greens of the trees in the distance. I used blue space-dyed fabric for the sky, which had white areas that looked like clouds. The bluebells are made from strips of blue, green and purple space-dyed fabric, placed and stitched following the rise of the hill. If you would like to reproduce the scene, start to stitch the sky with a swirl or wave pattern freehand, using the free machine embroidery foot. Remember to work from the centre out, starting between the two silver birch tree trunks. Work the sky and background trees before working the two main tree trunks. Continue working outwards and downwards. I placed the canopy of the silver birch tree in the foreground last, using very fine green chiffon, distressed and pulled to give the effect of the leaves on the branches, leaving holes for the sky to show through. This picture has been heavily machine stitched and embroidered with viscose threads, especially the markings on the tree trunks.

69

Summer

Foxgloves

This is the summer piece from my Forest of Dean quilt. It shows a bright summer's day with sun streaming through the trees, lighting up the woodland and casting dark shadows from the tree trunks. The beautiful foxgloves stand tall at the edge of the trees in the foreground of the picture, making a colourful display. Torn strips of space-dyed cotton were used for the ground, the tree trunks were appliquéd in cotton with that lovely pink hue and green chiffon was used for the branches. The foxglove leaves were appliquéd, and the flowers were machine embroidered with lots of detail.

Opposite

Poppy Fields

To me this picture shows the very essence of summer. I was travelling through Herefordshire with my camera at the ready, snapping any scene that looked promising for a textile landscape, when I suddenly saw a red hill in the distance. Tantalizingly, it vanished, so I had to wait, hoping it would come into sight again. The red was so vivid that I knew it had to be fields of poppies. Even though we were travelling to Scotland for our summer holiday, my husband made a detour to search for this elusive hill, and we travelled through many narrow country lanes trying to get to the poppies. The high hedges only gave us an occasional glimpse of them. I took photographs holding the camera high above my head, through holes in the hedge and from opposite hills. Roughly two hours later, we found them — what a wonderful sight! There were millions of dancing, bright red poppies which had grown and flowered after the rapeseed flowers had died.

When we returned from our holiday, I started the picture opposite. I had a piece of space-dyed fabric exactly right for the field: mainly red with some greens on the bottom edge. I did not need to change it much at all, except to overlay the main field area with red organza to made the red more vivid. I used a piece of blue space-dyed fabric for the sky and cut strips of different greens for the fields. May Hill in the distance and all the fields and hedges are machine stitched in straight stitch with different greens to show the distance. The distant buildings are machine stitched with white and greys; no fine detail is required as they are so far away.

The foreground on this picture is unusual; I let the dyed fabric dictate how I needed to stitch and it became more abstract. I hand stitched a few French knots in yellow to represent rapeseed flowers, using one, two or three strands of stranded embroidery cotton depending on the distance of the flowers into the picture. The moon daisies' centres are hand embroidered with yellow French knots, and the petals are stitched in white by machine. I used small circles of red organza and red viscose for the individual poppy heads, choosing either one or two layers, again depending on the flower's distance from the foreground. I machine stitched around each poppy head with dark green thread to make them stand out. I then beaded the centres with tiny black and dark purple iridescent glass beads.

Autumn

Autumn Oaks

This is the autumn landscape from my Forest of Dean quilt. This is the other side of the Cannop Ponds from the picture opposite. This view shows the bank of large oak trees, simply worked with cut shapes of space-dyed fabric. The water was made from dyed blue and white cotton overlaid with organza strips. I appliquéd the tree trunks and added chiffon leaves. I used lots of machine embroidery to give colour, light and shade with a wonderful palette of strong, vivid autumn tints.

Cannop Ponds

Three miles from where I live in the Forest of Dean, there is a lovely beauty spot called Cannop Ponds. The first and lower pond was built in 1825 to supply water to the Parkend Ironworks, to power a huge water wheel. There was still not enough water flow, so they built a dam alongside the embankment to make a second pond in 1829 to gain more water power. Now that this is no longer an industrial site, the peace and beauty of the scene gives pleasure to everyone who visits them.

Cannop Ponds is a very special place to me: it is where I took my children walking and one of my sons went fishing, and now I take my granddaughters to feed the ducks and swans. I have stitched many landscapes inspired by the beauty of the ponds, which I have tried to replicate at different times of year.

Autumn is my favourite season to photograph and stitch because of the vivid colours of the leaves on the wonderful trees surrounding the water. There are large oak trees for a wide area along the banks of the ponds, giving lots of walks and picnic areas, and you can walk right to the water's edge, enabling you to sketch, paint or take photographs.

I took the photograph that inspired the piece opposite on a beautiful sunny day, which made the colours glow. It looked as though the trees were on fire, and the reflection in the water returned the flames in a mirror image. In some areas, tall reeds stand at the edge of the ponds; there is a very dense area on the right-hand side of this picture and in the foreground, giving the picture depth. Some of the foreground reeds are standing tall in the water, their reflection showing as dark green, zigzag lines. This shows the movement of the water as it nears the outlet to travel on down the Cannop stream, eventually into the River Lyd then into the River Severn.

I space dyed my own base fabrics to achieve the vivid colour range, and in some areas I overlaid chiffons and organza to add extra shimmer and depth of colour. To give the water sparkle, I added small strips of metallic or crystal organza and stitched a few horizontal lines with metallic thread to give the illusion of sunlight reflecting on the water.

73

Winter

Tree in Snow

This grey winter scene is also from the Forest of Dean quilt. It has a very subdued colour palette: grey, black, purple and white. The water in the pond reflects the grey sky and there is a blanket of snow on the ground, leaving very little detail. This picture relies on the simplicity of the foreground tree, the subdued colours of the fabric, and very simple stitching.

Winter Fields

This is a scene I photographed on the way to Ross in Herefordshire. All the fields were covered with a blanket of snow, the light was quite dull and the sky leaden as if another storm was due. The trees in the nearest hedge looked very dark against the white snow, showing their skeletal branches reaching for the sky. The stalks of the harvested crop stood above the snow-covered ground, showing the lines where they had grown. The distant hill took on a blue haze, making all the fields and hedges in the distance look misty and pale greyish-blue. The foreground fields looked white or pale blue.

I dyed all the coloured fabrics for this piece myself. The different whites rely on the weave or mixed fibres of the fabrics to create the various effects. I started with the sky in a grey-blue fabric and the hills in a paler shade of the grey-blue. I then machine stitched all the distant hedges, and the outline of individual fields, in a pale grey-blue viscose machine embroidery thread. The large trees and the hedge on the eyeline are made from a dark green space-dyed fabric which has some paler areas, giving the effect of small amounts of snow on the trees. The third and fourth fields are stitched with straight stitching following the contours of the land. The second field from you is in white fabric, showing that the light source comes from the left. I stitched lines of straight machine stitching, in a white viscose thread, to show the perspective of how this field dips into the valley: the parallel lines get wider as they come towards you.

The main detail is concentrated in the white foreground field. I used very fine dark blue chiffon for the shadows, and lay small torn pieces of chiffon on to the field to show the rough, uneven surface. The lines of the corn stalks show the perspective of the land as it disappears down the hill into the valley, as the rows get narrower in the distance. I first machine stitched the lines in an irregular zigzag stitch in a medium brown, then hand embroidered over the lines with several shades of brown in a straight stitch, each stalk is an individual stitch. When stitching the stalks, remember that not all the stalks stand upright; some are at an angle, as this will give a more natural look.

Projects

This piece shows the New Forest National Park, Hampshire, an area of ancient forests and open heathland. I used the torn strip technique (see page 32) for the moorland area and the water's edge, simplified appliqué for the woodland area in the background and overlaid organza for the water. The two foreground trees were appliquéd, then heavily machine-embroidered for the details.

Autumn Woodland

Autumn in the Forest of Dean is magical, dressed in this amazing palette of colours. Set between the River Severn and the River Wye, the Forest is reputed to be 1000 years old, with large numbers of oak, beech, silver birch and many more deciduous trees, as well as conifers of many varieties. Autumn has always been the time for harvesting nature's bounty there: hazelnuts, blackberries, elderberries and chestnuts to cook in the embers of the open fire.

If you are born in the Forest within the Hundred of St Briavels, (which I was), there are Commoners' rights, allowing you to graze sheep there and let pigs roam free in the autumn. I have never claimed this right but in the past lots of families, including my parents, kept a pig in a garden pigsty.

The forest is full of magic and history and I never get tired of trying to reproduce its beauty in stitched landscapes.

You will need

- Shears and small, sharp-pointed scissors
- Mechanical pencil
- Tracing paper
- Paper scissors
- Light box
- Pins and needles
- Sewing machine
- Free machine embroidery foot
- Sewing machine embroidery needles
- 3 x bobbins for the machine
- Pale blue-grey viscose machine thread to fill the bobbins
- Iron, mini craft iron and baking parchment
- 2 pieces of white cotton fabric, 40 x 30cm (15¾ x 11¾in)
- Cotton wadding, 40 x 30cm (15¾ x 11¾in)
- Fusible web
- Blue and white space-dyed cotton, 40 x 20cm (15¾ x 8in)
- Orange space-dyed cotton, 40 x 15cm (15¾ x 6in)
- Brown and orange space-dyed fabric, 40 x 13cm (15¾ x 5in)
- Purple space-dyed cotton, 50 x 25cm (19¾ x 10in)
- Small pieces of grey space-dyed cotton for the fence
- Organza in shot orange/yellow, medium orange, bright orange, peach and yellow
- Chiffon in peach, bright orange and yellow
- Space-dyed scrim in green and brown
- Viscose machine embroidery threads: light, medium and bright orange, light, medium and dark purple, pale green, green and dark green, yellow, pale yellow, brown, maroon, cream, navy and white
- Silver metallic thread

1 I enlarged this 10 x 15cm (4 x 6in) photograph to A4 size on best photographic paper, then photocopied the A4 image in colour on to basic white copy paper on a text setting. Place tracing paper over the photocopy and trace the main design lines. I have moved the fence slightly to the right to get a better balance to the picture. Photocopy the tracing twice on to white photocopy paper to make your patterns.

2 Take one piece of the white cotton fabric and place it over the tracing on a light box. Trace the main lines on to the white fabric.

3 Trace the tree shapes on to fusible web using a mechanical pencil and remembering to turn your tracing over to the reverse side before placing it under the fusible web. Add at least an extra 2.5cm (1in) at the top of each tree. This will give you a reverse image on the fusible web backing paper. To save on the amount of fusible web, you can cut the branches of the large tree separately to the tree trunk.

4 I have divided the background into three main areas: sky, middle ground and foreground. Cut out the pattern on the main design lines. Lay the sky pattern on the blue space-dyed fabric, allowing 5mm (¼in) seam allowance at the lower edge and 2.5cm (1in) on the outside edges. Pin in place and cut the fabric around the extra seam allowance. Place the middle pattern on the orange space-dyed fabric, add a 5mm (¼in) seam allowance to the lower edge and 2.5cm (1in) to the two sides. Pin in place and cut out. Position the lower piece of pattern on the rich brown and orange space-dyed cotton, add a 2.5cm (1in) seam allowance to the bottom and the two sides. Pin and cut out.

5 Remove the paper patterns. Following the pencil guidelines on the white fabric, pin the three fabric pieces in place, overlapping the seam allowance as required. Tack with thread matching the fabric using a very small running stitch (the stitches will stay in.) Cut out the fusible web tree pattern, leaving extra fabric all the way around, rather than cutting out on the traced tree line. Place each piece face down on the tree fabric, with baking parchment underneath and on top. Press with a hot iron until the fusible web has adhered to the fabric. Wait until cool, then cut out tree shapes on the drawn lines (see inset).

Place a piece of baking parchment on the ironing board and place the picture right-side up on the baking parchment. Remove the backing from the tree shapes. Using your pencil lines for guidance, place the four trees in position, adhesive side down. Run the point of the mini craft iron down the centre of each tree, but leaving the edges of the trunks and the branches free. Later you will be able to stitch under them, which creates a more realistic finish.

6 Cut and distress small uneven pieces of orange, yellow, shot orange/yellow and peach organza and chiffon. Gather parts of the fabric and pull to make holes in other parts. Following the photograph, lay the distressed pieces on your landscape to look like the branches and leaves. Position the long main branch, make sure there is baking parchment underneath and touch the branch with the point of the mini craft iron, taking care not to touch the organza or chiffon, as it may melt. Lay some of the organza and chiffon over the trunk and branch, leaving some areas showing through.

Cut a long thin piece of green scrim for the grass, with uneven edges, and two pieces of brown scrim for the undergrowth, suggesting dead leaves. Add more pieces to give depth of colour and interest.

For the tree trunks, place thin strips of very dark purple scrim down the shadowed right-hand side. Place strips of green scrim on the left-hand sides of the tree trunks to represent the growth of moss. Pin all the distressed fabrics in place and hand stitch with a small running stitch in matching threads, leaving the edges of the tree trunks free.

Note

Before beginning the free machine embroidery, think about how you need to stitch each section. Always work away from the last stitching you did, rather than towards it, as you may get surplus fabric puffing up in between.

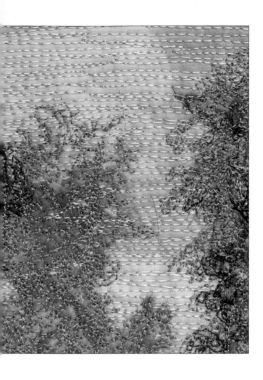

7 Take the second piece of white cotton fabric and lay it on the work surface. Place the wadding on top and the fabric picture on top of that, right side up. Pin and tack through all thicknesses in a grid shape, working from the middle out.

Prepare the machine for free machine embroidery as shown on page 34. Start to machine stitch, working the area between the centre tree and the far left tree trunk. Stitch the sky with pale blue thread in straight horizontal lines and the leaves in peach and pale orange, using circular movements. Change colours as necessary. Lift the edges of both tree trunks to enable you to stitch under the edge; this will give a better finish.

8 Now work the central tree trunk. Stitch with light, dark and medium purples, green for the moss, dark navy for the shadows and white for the highlights. Leave the right-hand edge of the tree trunk free of stitching to enable you to stitch leaves and branches underneath it as before.

Note

At this stage, work the sky and tree sections as far as the large horizontal branch. Do not yet complete the tree trunks.

9 Now stitch between the central tree and the right-hand tree. Work as before, leaving some areas between the branches for the sky to show through. Now you can finish stitching the edge of the central tree trunk.

10 Complete the stitching on the left-hand side of the fourth, right-hand tree trunk with pale green and pale purple threads. Leave the right-hand side of the trunk free so that you can stitch underneath it when working the next section of background foliage.

11 Stitch the final section of the right-hand background trees and sky. Complete the right-hand edge of the tree trunk, but do not stitch the lower half of the trunk. Stitch the tree branch with dark and medium purple thread for the shadow areas and pale purple where the light catches the branch.

12 Return to the left-hand side of picture and complete the tree trunks and background as before. Stitch the distant silver birch trunks in pale lilac and use a darker purple for the background trees on the left.

13 Stitch the branch that sweeps across the foreground and then the leaves, stitching in circular movements with various oranges and greens. Make sure you leave some areas of the tree trunks showing, working the trunks for the first two trees and the centre section of the middle tree as you go.

Work the bottom section of the central tree trunk, leaving both edges free as before. Now work the ground section between the central and right-hand trees. Lift the edges of the tree trunks so that the stitching can go underneath. Now work the right-hand tree trunk, leave the right-hand edge free. Stitch the background area, then finish the fourth tree trunk.

Go back to the central trunk, finish the background then complete the stitching on the left-hand side of the central tree trunk.

14 For the distant ground, work with upright stitching to represent young silver birch trees in mauves, with green for long grass.

In the middle ground, stitch upright with light, medium and dark greens for the grass, with brown in circular movements and some straight lines for dead leaves. Use dark purple and navy for the shadows of the trees.

In the foreground, use light green for the upright grass with some lines in green, orange, brown and rust.

15 Trace the fence posts and struts in reverse on to fusible web backing paper. Iron them on to the back of a small piece of space-dyed grey cotton fabric. Cut out the fence posts, using your design tracing, and position them on your work. You will need to adjust the size because the amount of stitching will have shrunk your work. Check that your fence posts and the spaces between them get smaller as they go away from you; this will create perspective in your picture. Remove the backing paper, cover the work with baking parchment and press the pieces in place with the tip of the hot iron. Stitch the posts and struts with dark purple and navy for the shadowed right-hand side and green for the left-hand side. With silver thread, machine the top and bottom wires. I have not put in any more detail of the wire to avoid the work becoming too cluttered.

Go back and add more stitching to the leaves so that they overlap the foreground and tree trunks to give a more natural look. Finally sign your name.

The finished picture.

Memories of Happy Days

This picture has played an important part in my life. I painted the scene many years ago when my children were young, and it has hung on my living room wall ever since. This beautiful area is about two miles from where I live and I have taken many photographs in recent years and produced several textile pictures, including the Autumn Woodland project itself.

1996 was a dreadful year for my family: my husband Derek died in France of a heart attack, and eight months later I fell on my icy garden path, breaking my ankle badly. I had no idea how difficult it was to be on crutches; you cannot even carry a cup of coffee. After a few weeks I was getting exasperated at the inactivity, so I asked my sons to get me some of my bags of space-dyed fabrics. I sat in my armchair surrounded with bits of fabric, wondering what I could do. My painting of the bluebell wood was on the wall in front of me so it was the obvious choice, and I had to try to create this scene. Sitting in an armchair with my leg elevated, I found it very difficult to cut the fabric with scissors. I managed to snip and tear one piece for the background. I was trying to replicate a painting and noticed that thin, torn pieces of fabric looked like brush strokes. I then chose an area of colour on one of the fabrics and tore a narrow strip. I carried on, cutting and tearing the different colours as required for the bluebells and the pathway. I pinned it all in place, then hand stitched with tiny running stitches using matching thread. This was the start of my torn strip technique (see page 32). With difficulty I cut out the tree trunks, then added little pieces of cream and coloured scrim overlaid on to the trunks for shadows and highlights. I then distressed part of a green chiffon scarf for the branches and leaves. The picture had taken many weeks of frustration to achieve, due to a lack of concentration from the pain and the physical difficulty of handling the fabrics and basic sewing equipment. Finally I was able to put my foot to the ground and with difficulty I managed to use my sewing machine. I heavily machine stitched and embroidered with viscose threads. To complete the picture I decided to bind the edges, making it look like the frame of the painting that had inspired me.

I called the picture 'Memories of Happy Days' after the many happy times Derek, our three sons and I walked through this wood at bluebell time.

My friend asked me if any good had come out of all the bad which had happened to me, to which I answered quite vehemently NO! The following May, the picture was entered into the Malvern Quilt Show, and although I was still on crutches, I had to take back the 'no' and tell her that I had come second for: 'the most exciting use of the sewing machine'. I was then invited by the Patchwork Association at the European Quilt Championships in Holland, to exhibit this piece at the show. Best of all I now had a new way of working which I have used on numerous pieces of work, winning more awards.

As they say, invention is born of necessity.

Flower Garden

We travelled to Oxfordshire to visit the annual international craft fair, Art in Action, which is held in the beautiful grounds of Waterperry House. This is a coming together of around four hundred top craft people, teachers and performers, demonstrating textiles, glass, jewellery, painting and dancing. It was a very hot summer day as we walked in and out of each marquee, in awe of the amazing work, and the colour and beauty of all the items on display. We all agreed it was an inspirational day.

Later in the afternoon we went to view the beautiful gardens, which are said to be among the finest in Oxfordshire. We strolled through the grounds, admiring the flowers, which I would describe as typical of English country garden borders. I took lots of photographs from different angles, trying to visualise the best compositions that would be suitable for textile pictures. It was close to my own dream garden. I would love a walled garden with huge borders of large herbaceous flowers, with lots of smaller flowers at the edges of the pathways and lawns. The final touch would be climbing roses and clematis against the walls.

A perfect garden would have flowers blooming and coloured foliage throughout the year, giving interest and colour. In reality, borders always have areas of foliage where the blooms have already flowered and died back, while other plants may not be ready to flower. I wanted to create a picture of a perfect garden full of flowers, even though this is not realistic. I have one main photograph of the Waterperry House garden, and have then lifted plants from a photograph of another area of the garden and interspersed them with the flowers on my original choice, to give lots of colour and shapes.

I worked the flowers with free machine embroidery, although they can be worked with hand embroidery or a mixture of both if you prefer. I hope you enjoy working this garden. You may wish to change the individual flowers to your own choice of plants from your garden, or maybe your own ideal dream garden.

You will need

- **Shears and small, sharp-pointed scissors**
- **Paper scissors**
- **Soft pastels and fixative**
- **Mechanical pencil**
- **Light box and tracing paper**
- **Pins and needles**
- **Sewing machine**
- **Free machine embroidery foot**
- **Appliqué or wide open-toed foot**
- **3 bobbins for the machine**
- **Light blue viscose thread to fill the bobbins**
- **2 pieces of white cotton fabric, 40 x 30cm (15¾ x 11¾in)**
- **Cotton wadding, 40 x 30cm (15¾ x 11¾in)**
- **Small piece of blue and white space-dyed cotton fabric, 10 x 30cm (4 x 11¾in)**
- **Small piece of brick-coloured cotton fabric**
- **Light pink-beige space-dyed cotton fabric, 20 x 13cm (8 x 5in)**
- **Space-dyed green cotton fabric, 45 x 30cm (17¾ x 11¾in)**
- **Small amounts of green space-dyed scrim**
- **Chiffon and viscose, small amounts of mauve, pink, yellow and green**
- **White lace, 20cm (8in)**
- **Viscose machine embroidery threads: light, medium and dark greens, yellows, purples, pinks, reds, beige, brick red, silver grey, medium grey, ecru, cream, aubergine, light brown and white**
- **Tacking cotton**

1 I took this 10 x 15cm (4 x 6in) print of a garden scene and enlarged it to A4 size, then chose the section shown, and enlarged that to A4, on to photographic paper.

2 I took this second photograph from the same garden and enlarged it on to A4 photographic paper in the same way. I then made a colour photocopy of each A4 image. I took the photocopy of the image from step 1, and used soft pastels to colour in areas, using the flowers from the other image as inspiration. I sprayed the picture with fixative, and photocopied the final design. I traced the outlines on to tracing paper, and photocopied the tracing to use as a pattern.

3 Use a pencil to trace the pattern on to your white cotton fabric on the light box.

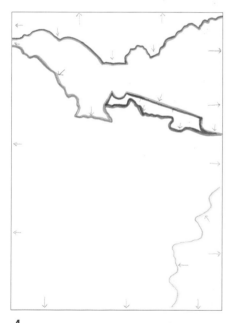

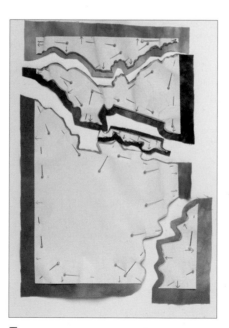

4 Mark the pattern with the various areas to cut out, with arrows for the seam allowances.

5 Cut out all the paper pattern pieces. Lay each pattern piece on to suitable coloured fabric and pin them in place. Cut out each shape, leaving a 5mm (¼in) seam allowance where indicated and 2.5cm (1in) all round the outside edges.

6 Remove the pattern pieces one at a time, and starting at the top of the sky, position the fabric pieces on the white fabric background. Pin them in place, then tack them with the same coloured thread as the fabric, using a very small stitch on top and a larger stitch on the reverse. These stitches will not be removed.

7 Take some of the pale green scrim, distress it by pulling holes in it and gathering it, and add it to the trees area to give depth and texture. Pin it in place. Choose relevant coloured chiffons to represent flowers and pin these in place. Cut small pieces of lace and position these for the white plants. Cut small pieces of pink viscose and yellow chiffon for the foreground flowers and pin these in place. When you are satisfied with the effect, tack all the fabrics in place with thread in the same colours and small stitches. Remove the pins. Make a wadding sandwich, starting by placing one piece of white cotton fabric on the table. Place the wadding on the cotton. Place the picture right side up on the wadding and pin and tack the layers together in a grid shape, working from the centre outwards.

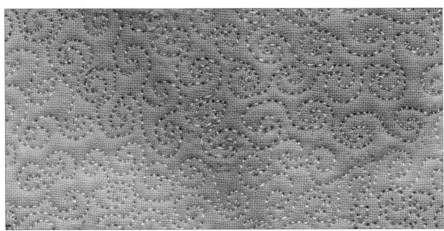

8 Prepare the sewing machine for free machine embroidery as shown on page 34. Wind at least three bobbins with light blue thread ready for when required. Thread the machine with medium blue viscose thread for the sky, place the bobbin in the bobbin case and pull the bobbin thread through. Free machine stitch the sky using a continuous swirl pattern as shown.

9 To create the trees, stitch with green thread, changing colours as necessary and working from the centre outwards, using random circular movements to give the effect of leaves. Note that if the scrim or chiffon becomes caught in the machine foot, do not worry, just cut the offending thread and continue.

10 To work the wall, change the machine foot to an open-toed foot, lift the dogteeth back up, change the stitch length back to normal and thread the machine with a medium grey viscose thread. Stitch along the wall in straight lines that gradually become closer together in the distance. This will give perspective and distance to your picture.

11 At this stage you may find that the fabric below your stitching begins to bubble up. If this happens, snip the tacking as you work your way down so that your work stays flat. Replace the foot with a free machine embroidery foot, change the stitch length to 0 and drop or cover the dogteeth. Continue working down the garden from the centre outwards, changing thread colours as required. Stitch with circular movements except for the purple, centre yellow and tall white plants, where you need to use an up and down movement to represent the stems. For the pink and yellow flowers in the foreground, stitch around the circles of fabric which represent the flower heads to hold them in place. Continue until all the picture is in place. Lay your original flower tracing on top of your work to help you position the flowers. Now start to stitch in the main details, again working from the top middle to the sides. Add more detail to the trees if required.

12 Using light brown thread, stitch the pillars on the brick wall. Stitch the climbing roses using green for the stems and white and red for the flowers.

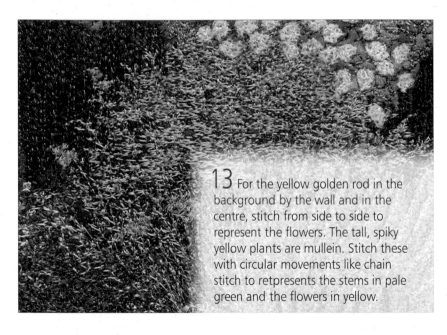

13 For the yellow golden rod in the background by the wall and in the centre, stitch from side to side to represent the flowers. The tall, spiky yellow plants are mullein. Stitch these with circular movements like chain stitch to retpresents the stems in pale green and the flowers in yellow.

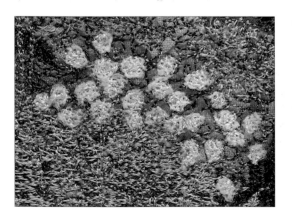

14 For the white roses, cut small circles of white lace and stitch them down with white thread. Stitch in a circular motion to create the effect of roses.

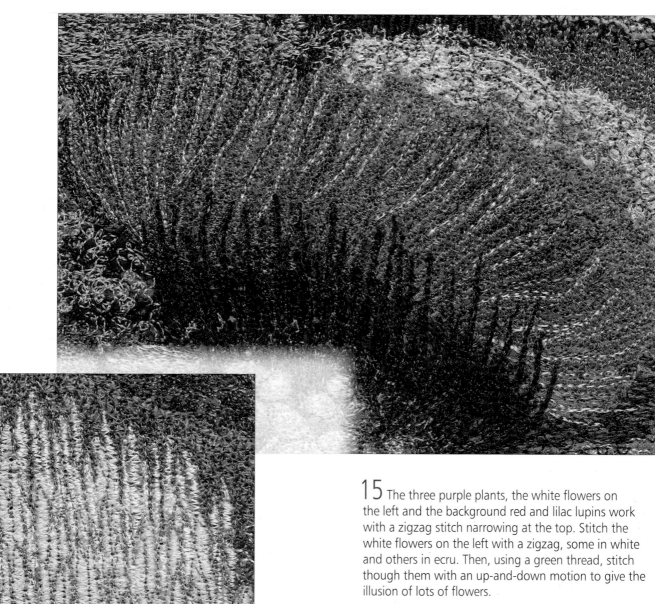

15 The three purple plants, the white flowers on the left and the background red and lilac lupins work with a zigzag stitch narrowing at the top. Stitch the white flowers on the left with a zigzag, some in white and others in ecru. Then, using a green thread, stitch though them with an up-and-down motion to give the illusion of lots of flowers.

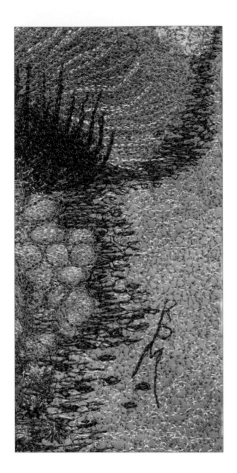

16 For the shadow on the path, use aubergine thread because the path has a pinkish shade; black would be much too dark. Use beige and ecru for the small stones.

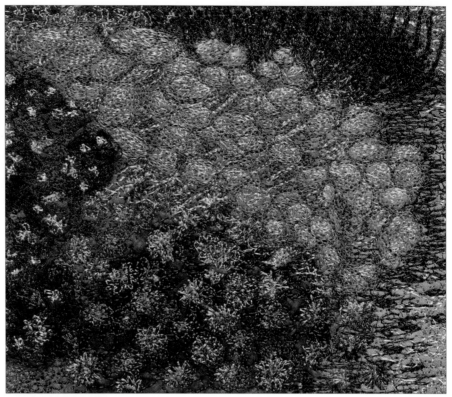

17 For the large yellow flowers in the foreground, use light, medium and dark yellow thread to stitch the flower heads. Stitch the stems in silver grey, then finally stitch with green thread round the heads to outline them, making them stand out. For the purple daisies, use three purples and pointed stitching to look like lots of small petals. Finish with a yellow centre. For the large pink flowers at bottom left, stitch the leaves first as they are in the background. I used a random green thread, stitching pointed leaves with a straight stitch. The flowers are stitched with three shades of pink: light, medium and dark, plus white. They are made up from lots of individual flower heads. Work each colour separately: move from head to head, then repeat with the other colours. Finally outline the large head with dark green stitching, moving randomly in between the small flower heads. Look at your work to see if it is buckling; it may need more stitching in some areas to flatten it. Finally remember to sign you work.

Opposite
The finished picture.

Peace and Tranquillity

This is a large picture, 61 x 52cm (24 x 20½in.) It shows water lilies under the shade of the trees, which give dappled shading on the large lily pads. They were made from space-dyed green cotton, with the stitching radiating outwards to the edges of the lily pad. The lily blossoms were each cut from one piece of space-dyed pink cotton fabric. The shape relies on the stitching to separate each petal, and the light and shade were stitched with light, medium and dark cerise pink, with highlights in white. The very dark shadow gives a strong accent in dark purple. The water was made from strips of organza in many colours, overlaid for the shadow with distressed chiffon.

96

Anticipation

In this picture we have many more exotic flowers. In the background is a bougainvillea climbing plant with beautiful magenta bracts which look like flowers, and dainty green leaves. The leaves were individually made from space-dyed cotton, the bracts from space-dyed cerise Habotai silk. The banana plant has huge leaves, again made from space-dyed cotton. I cut the leaves so that the light and dark areas of the dyed cotton complement each one, giving the illusion of the sun shining through the garden.

Mountain Lake

We were holidaying in the beautiful Lake District in England, where the scenery is magnificent. Most of the roads were very narrow and steep, with death-defying hairpin bends. My husband drove the car while I tried to take photographs with my small point-and-shoot camera, through an open side window, or through the windscreen. This was not easy; as we twisted and turned, the view I wanted often disappeared. This photograph was obviously taken on a good piece of road with a clear view.

For this project I have only used the top right-hand section of the picture. Look at the wonderful array of colours visible in the mountains: pale blue, dark blue, purple, pink, green and very dark green. I could not wait to convey something of this beautiful scene in fabric and stitch.

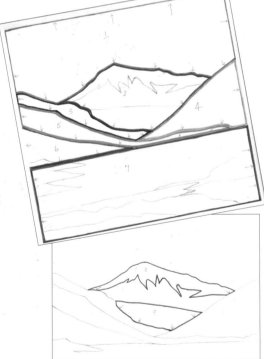

1 I enlarged a 10 x 15cm (4 x 6in) print of this mountainous scene to A4 on best quality photographic paper, then chose the area shown and enlarged this to A4, again on photographic paper. I then traced this image using tracing paper, and photocopied it twice to make the patterns for this piece.

2 I added to the depth of the sky to make the image more pleasing, then created these patterns, with numbers to show the order of work and arrows to show seam allowances. Top left is the main pattern, above left are the shadows on the mountain and above right are the rocks and other foreground features.

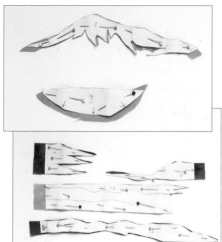

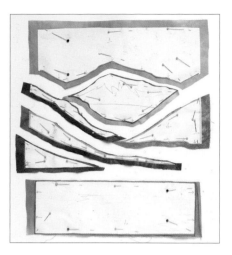

3 Lay the pattern on the light box and trace the design on to your white background fabric.

4 Cut out the paper pattern pieces. Choose suitable coloured cotton fabrics and navy organza for the mountain shadows. Add seam allowances of 5mm (¼in), and 2.5cm (1in) round the outside edges, as shown by the arrows. Pin the paper pieces in place and cut out all the pieces with scissors, apart from the top of the water where torn cotton gives a good effect.

5 Start to lay your fabric pieces on to the backing fabric, beginning with the sky. Work your way downwards, overlapping the seam allowances. Pin as you go. Take your organza fabrics for the water and tear into 1.5cm (½in) or 2.5cm (1in) strips as required, following the picture (see detail above right). Use the colours to create shadows, lights and darks and overlay to get secondary colours. Where you have torn the organza, the theads will gather up to give you a greater density. When you are happy with the results, pin in place. Position the rocks and foreground and pin. Place the mountain shadow, no. 8, pin it in place with the two ends tucked in under the other mountains. Place piece no. 9 and tuck the seam allowance under the mountains (see detail, right). Pin in place. Hand stitch all the edges in place, working from the top downwards, using a small stitch on top and a long stitch on the back, with matching thread. Remove the pins as you go. Make a wadding sandwich (see above right) with backing white cotton at the bottom, wadding on top of that, then your picture right side up. Pin all the layers together and tack in a grid as shown above, left.

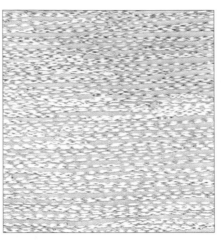

6 Set your machine for free machine embroidery (see page 34) and thread it with blue thread which matches the sky fabric. Start machining the sky at the centre top, working your way outwards and downwards, randomly changing to grey-blue, lighter blue or white thread to give depth and movement in the sky. Work as far as the top of the central mountain, then stop.

7 Start to work on the central mountain. Do not be tempted to finish the sky before starting the mountain. Following the general rule, start to work the mountain from the centre, gradually working outwards and downwards in straight stitch. Use navy blue, dark blue and dark grey-toned blue for the shadows and pale pink and light blue-toned green for the lighter areas. Go back to the sky and finish either side of the mountain.

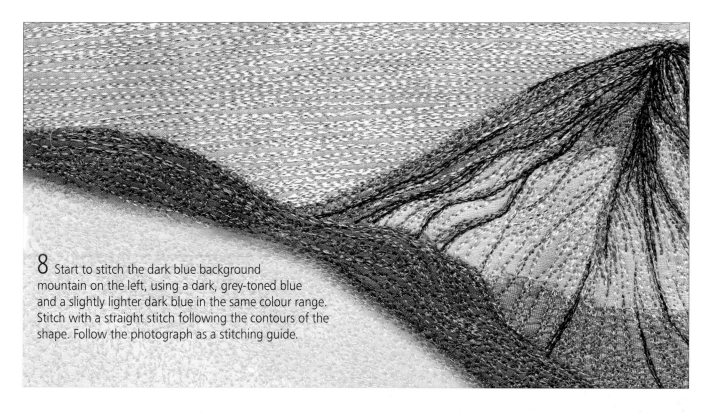

8 Start to stitch the dark blue background mountain on the left, using a dark, grey-toned blue and a slightly lighter dark blue in the same colour range. Stitch with a straight stitch following the contours of the shape. Follow the photograph as a stitching guide.

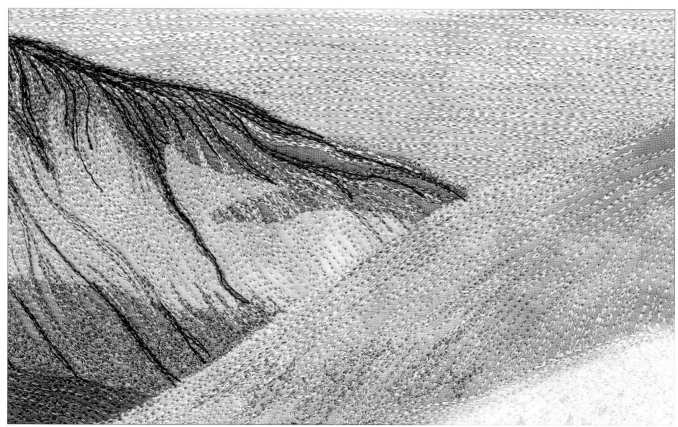

9 Next, work the light green, sun-drenched mountain on the right. Use a pale yellow-green, pale pink, medium blue-green, yellow-toned green and light beige. Continue stitching until level with the bottom of the dark green mountain, then stop. Do not complete the remaining small area of the pale green mountain to the right of the picture.

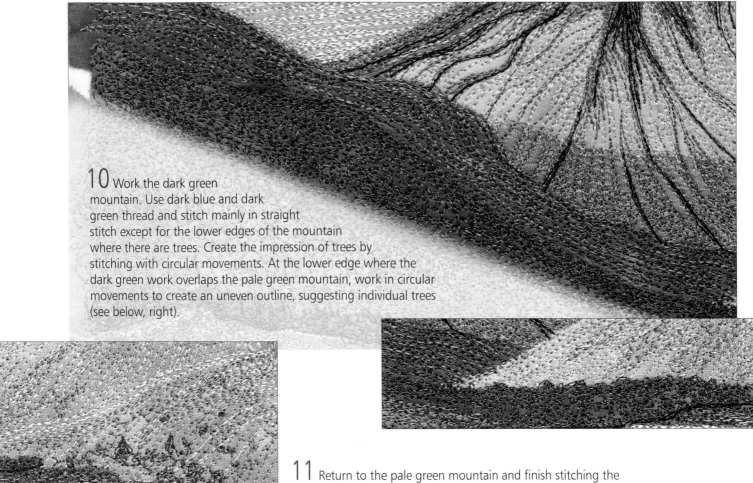

10 Work the dark green mountain. Use dark blue and dark green thread and stitch mainly in straight stitch except for the lower edges of the mountain where there are trees. Create the impression of trees by stitching with circular movements. At the lower edge where the dark green work overlaps the pale green mountain, work in circular movements to create an uneven outline, suggesting individual trees (see below, right).

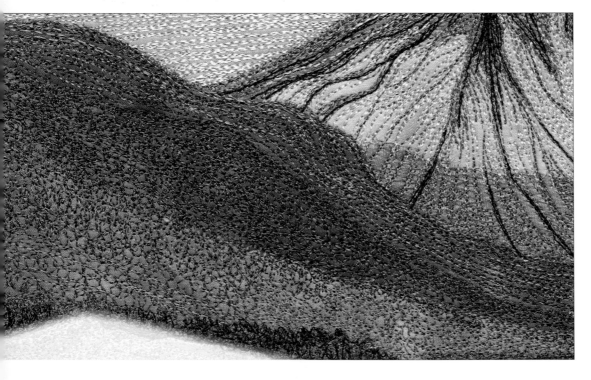

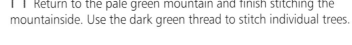

11 Return to the pale green mountain and finish stitching the mountainside. Use the dark green thread to stitch individual trees.

12 Stitch the lower part of the dark green mountain on the left. Using navy, dark blue and dark green thread, work with a circular movement where there are trees and with straight stitch following the slopes down to the water's edge. At the lower edge of this area, there are lines of very dark fir trees. Use the navy thread and a circular movement to represent them. Outline the bottom edge of the mountain, working some trees as you go. To the right of the lower edge, the navy line moves upwards to denote the end of the tree line (see opposite page, top).

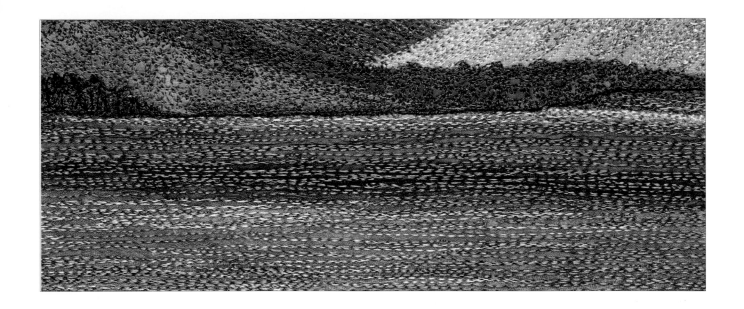

13 Working from the centre out, start to stitch the water (above) using dark, medium and pale grey-toned blue. The important rule is to keep the stitching of the water level in line with the top and bottom edges of the picture. The rule changes at the bottom of the pale green mountain, as the shoreline moves towards you. Gradually blend in the colours, using the same method as for the sky. Work the three sections of land on the left at the same time (see left), with three yellow-toned greens plus navy, and for the rock section, rose pink, light pink-toned brown and beige plus navy. Change threads as necessary. Work the land on the right-hand side (see below) in medium green, pink, light green, light pink-toned brown, beige, and dark brown.

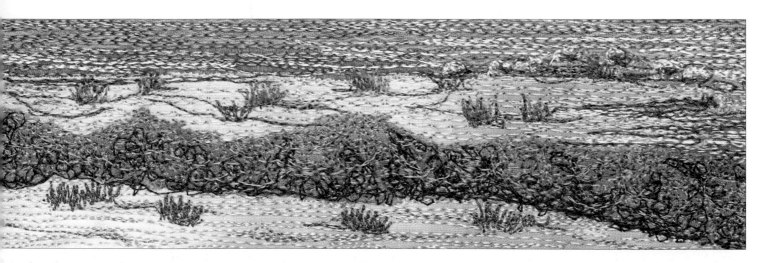

14 When you get to the foreground, stop working on the water and start to stitch the land in the same way as before, changing colours when required. Use light medium and dark green, light pink-toned brown and navy.

15 Complete the water on the right-hand side of the picture, where it is flowing over pebbles and small rocks. Stitch in the small rocks with grey, beige and brown, using circular movements. Remember that the darker parts, the shadows, should be on the right.

16 When you have finished the basic colours of all the water, work the white line in the distance on the water's edge to show the reflected light. At the bottom of the right-hand mountain, use a beige thread. For the running water at the bottom, create the reflected light and movement using silver metallic thread, and for the shadows, pink-toned brown and brown. Finally, check that you are happy with your work and add more stitching if necessary, then sign the piece.

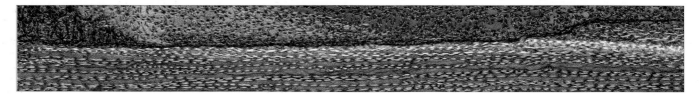

The finished picture.

Through the Valley

Each time we return to this beautiful area in the Lake District, I marvel again at its magnificent scenery.

I was due to demonstrate at the Exeter Quilt Show, when I photographed this scene. I chose this photograph out of the many I took to recreate in fabric. I constructed the picture with torn strips of space-dyed fabric, using purples, greens, blues and the lovely russet tones of autumn. The only exceptions to the torn strip method (see page 32) are the distant mountain top, which I cut to shape, and the trees in the valley. To show the contours of the fields, hills and mountains, I manipulated the torn strips to bend and curve, giving the shapes needed for both gentle and steep slopes. I added more detail to the fields, distant hedges and foreground grassland with machine embroidery stitching. I also machine embroidered clumps of reed-like plants and the distant sheep grazing on the slopes, to give extra interest. I stitched the small river horizontally to show the way the water meanders and tumbles downwards between the hills and onwards through the valley.

Sunset Loch

On holiday in Scotland, we had been to visit the beautiful Isle of Mull. We were traveling back from the Island after a wonderful day exploring and photographing. We had hoped to catch the ferry back across Loch Linnhe, to the Fort William side of the loch, but we were too late. We now had a long drive ahead of us, so we decided to have our evening meal at the inn opposite the ferry slipway. When we had finished eating, we went out to the car. The sun was just setting and the golden light turned Loch Linnhe and the sky into a beautiful wonderland. I was mesmerised and took countless photographs to capture the moment.

The picture I chose to turn into a stitched landscape showed this wonderful sunset just as I remembered it. The sky had beautiful pinks, peaches, blues and golds, with the water reflecting the colour back to the sky. The backdrop of misty blue mountains and the jet-black rocky foreground made it look very dramatic.

To capture this magical scene, I worked the picture with organzas and my own space-dyed cotton. I kept the stitching very simple, using free machine straight line stitching and contour lines to emphasise the simplicity of the lines in the water, sky, mountains and rocky foreground. This allowed the fabrics to work their magic, replicating the colours of this wonderful evening landscape.

Even though we had a long detour, we were pleased we had missed the ferry; not only did we see this magnificent sunset, we also saw an elusive pine marten crossing the road, then two stags with full antlers in a moonlit field, full of beautiful white moon daisies. The extra miles were definitely worthwhile.

You will need

Shears, small, sharp-pointed scissors and paper scissors with sharp points

Mechanical pencil and light box

Pins and needles

Sewing machine with free machine embroidery foot and 3 bobbins

Sewing machine embroidery needles

Pale grey-blue viscose machine thread to fill the bobbins

Iron and baking parchment

2 pieces of white cotton fabric, 40 x 30cm (15¾ x 11¾in)

Cotton wadding, 40 x 30cm (15¾ x 11¾in)

Dark grey-blue space-dyed fabric with different shaded areas, 40 x 15cm, (15¾ x 6in)

Black cotton fabric, 30 x 23cm (11¾ x 9in)

Blue organza, 40.6 x 30cm (16 x 11¾in)

Organza strips, peach and pale gold, 40.6 x 15cm (16 x 6in)

Crystal organza, white, gold, silver-grey and pale gold, 40.6 x 15cm (16 x 6in)

Viscose machine embroidery threads to match fabrics: white, black, blue, peach, gold, pale gold and silver-grey

Tacking cotton

Narrow black ribbon, 150cm (60in)

1 I enlarged a 10 x 15cm (4 x 6in) print of this scene to A4 size on photographic paper, then photocopied this on ordinary paper. I then traced the main design lines on to tracing paper, and photocopied the tracing to make a paper pattern. I marked numbers for the various sections and the order in which they should be placed, as well as adding arrows for 5mm (¼in) seam allowances, and 2.5cm (1in) around the edges.

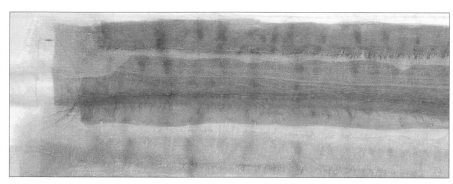

2 Using a light box, transfer the design on to white cotton fabric. Cut out your paper pattern and lay each piece on to suitably coloured fabric. Cut out each piece carefully, including the seam allowances. I like to lay out the pieces in order beside the fabric, so that I can see where everything goes.

3 Tear strips of organza from 1.5cm (½in) to 2.5cm (1in) wide. Lay them on to the sky area from top to bottom, matching the colours in the photograph, starting with blue, then grey, then white, then peach. Continue with the peach, crystal white, crystal gold, then pale gold. Overlap the edges to get wonderful secondary colours. When you are happy with the arrangement, pin in place.

4 Cut out three hills from the dark grey-blue space-dyed fabric. Lay them in place, following the order on the pattern and overlapping at the seam allowances. Pin in place. Cut out, place and pin the fourth hill, on the right, in the same way.

5 For the water, tear strips of organza as before in blue, silver-grey, white and gold. Keep looking at the photograph and comparing the colours. Lay the first piece of organza so that it overlaps the bottom of the hill. This creates the effect of a reflection. Continue downwards, overlapping the strips to create secondary colours. In the foreground, overlap the pencil lines where the black silhouette will go. When you are happy with the arrangement, pin in place.

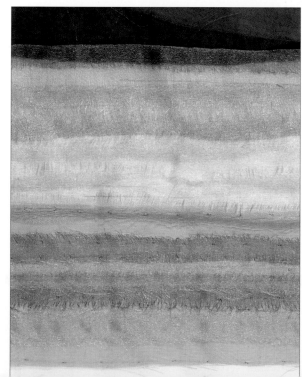

109

6 The last piece to lay in place is the black foreground. Tuck the top edge under the water organza, then pin the rest on top of the organza. When you are happy with the effect, tack all the fabrics in place, using threads to match each one. Use a small stitch on top and a long stitch underneath, as these stitches will stay in place. You may get stray organza threads; just cut them off.

7 Take a second piece of white cotton fabric and lay it flat on the table. Place the cotton wadding on top, then your tacked picture, face up. Pin all three layers together and tack in a grid pattern as shown, using tacking cotton, working from the centre outwards.

8 Thread the machine with blue viscose thread and prepare it for free machine embroidery, as shown on page 34. Starting at the top of the sky, stitch a straight line from one side to the other. Turn the picture round and stitch back to the other side, very close to the other line. If you do not feel confident stitching freehand, replace the foot with the normal straight stitch

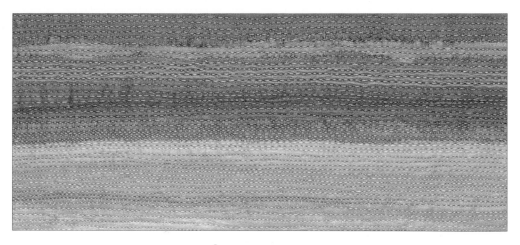

foot and lift the dogteeth up. Do not worry about little wobbles, as nature does not have completely straight lines. Continue down to the top of the mountains, changing threads to match the sky fabric. Lift the edges of the mountain fabric and stitch underneath. Complete the centre of the sky.

9 Next work the mountains. The colour depth on the mountains changes from light to dark as they come forward. Starting with the furthest away, reset your machine for zigzag with the dogteeth up. Stitch the edge of the most distant mountain using a narrow width with 05 setting for satin stitch. Finish the stitching by lifting the mountain on the right and machining underneath. Reset the machine to straight stitch and stitch lines following the shape of the mountain. At the end of each line, lift the edge of the next area to hide the stitched

ends. Continue by stitching the right-hand mountain in the same way, matching thread to fabric, followed by the third then fourth mountain on the left, coming forwards.

10 Begin on the water. Turn under the top edge of the blue organza, stitch it in place by hand using small stitches, then top stitch it in place by machine. The blue organza overlaying the mountain fabric will give the impression of reflections of the mountains in the water.

11 Stitch the water in the same way as the sky, hiding the ends of your lines of stitching under the black fabric. When you have stitched approximately 4cm (1½in) down from the top of the water, stop, re-thread the machine with black thread, change to the machine foot, put the dogteeth up and set the machine for zigzag. Stitch the edge of the black bank fabric until you are level with the last row of water stitching. Change the foot and machine settings back to free machine stitching. Contour the black areas in the same way as you did the mountains, until level with the last row of water stitching. Continue stitching the water, changing the colour of thread as before. Stop again after stitching approximately another 4cm (1½in) down. Reset the machine for zigzag stitch, re-thread in black and stitch the bank edge. Continue in this way until the water and bank are finished. With black thread, stitch some lines at the water's edge to represent reflections. Stitch in circular movements to represent small rocks.

12 At this point I used the colour photocopy taken in step 1 to help get the angles of the railings right, to create perspective. Place black ribbons into position for the railings and tack them in place. Set the machine for straight stitch and machine the ribbon in place at the top and bottom edges. Position and pin the railing posts, making sure the spaces between each post decrease as the rails go away from you. Machine them in place.

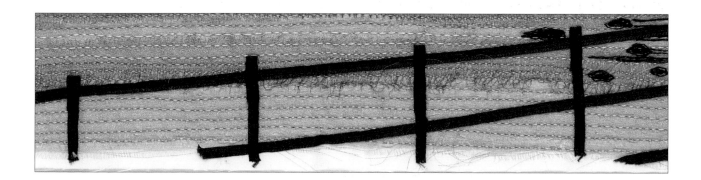

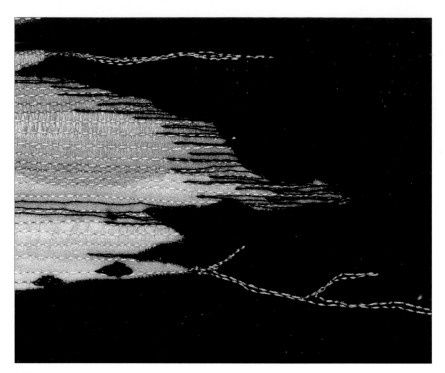

13 Reset the machine for free machine embroidery, thread with pale blue thread and stitch the small details into the black area to give the impression of water inlets. Check that your work is flat, and if not, do more stitching into the area that has bubbled. Finally sign your name.

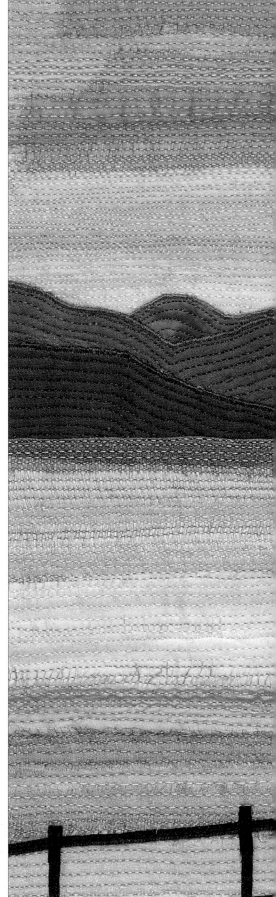

The finished picture.

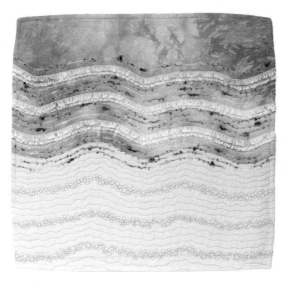 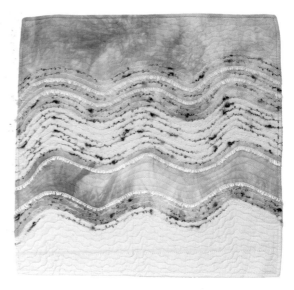

These three pieces belong to a set of five textiles showing a more abstract way of representing water and pebbles at the water's edge. The water was made from the same large piece of space-dyed cotton (see page 47). The movement of the water was made from a fringed knitting yarn and a second knitting yarn of textured white threads with gathered fibres of different blues caught into the twist of the yarn. The yarn gives added interest to the water. The cream areas are soft calico machine stitched with wavy contour lines to represent the shorelines. In the top left-hand and bottom pictures, the effect of the shingle or tiny pebbles was machine stitched, following the contour lines and stitching in continuous circles. In the top left-hand picture, every other row of fringed yarn has been trimmed shorter, and in the top right-hand picture, all the rows of fringed yarn have been trimmed.

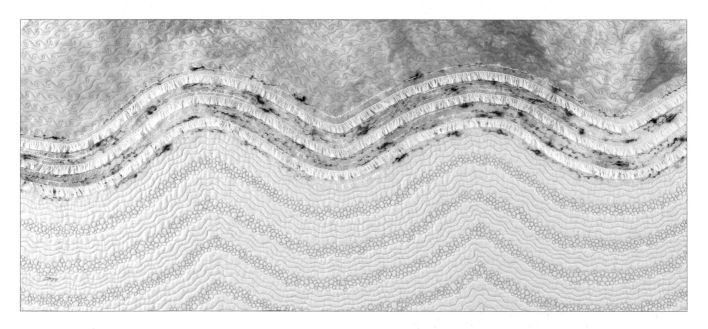

Opposite

Waterfall

I photographed this waterfall on holiday in Scotland. As my husband, Dave, and I approached it, the grass began to sink beneath our feet. I eventually managed to take the photograph I wanted, but we had a hilarious time and both ended up with soaking wet feet.

The stormy sky was made with space-dyed blue and white cotton. The top section was overlaid with strips of different shades of blue and navy organza. For the lower section, I placed very fine black chiffon that has been distressed to make it look like the storm clouds. The sky was then heavily machine stitched with many different shades of blue from turquoise to navy. The lower section of clouds was stitched with grey shades from mauves and blues, then cream. The bottom of the sky was stitched with blue and white. The distant mountain was made from dark blue space-dyed fabric, and the hills from different shades of green, overlaid with dyed scrim to give texture. The rocky hillside at the top is in shadow, so space-dyed cotton was overlaid with very fine black chiffon, then areas were cut back to let the colour show through. The lower rocks were made from lighter blue-grey space-dyed cotton. The water was made from two pieces of white crystal organza fused together with fusible web between two sheets of baking parchment. Be careful not to melt the organza with too hot an iron. I cut out the shape of the water from the organza, positioned it on the picture and placed baking parchment on top before pressing with the hot iron. All areas were heavily machine embroidered. I stitched the water with white viscose thread and added a little silver metallic thread to give more sparkle. The lower rocks were done using the colours in the space-dyed fabric. I encircled each area several times to make the rocks stand out. The water flows around the rocks. I added srim to some of the outside rocks to look like moss.

117

Lavender Farm

I have always admired photographs of the fields of lavender in Provence, France. We visited a small lavender farm when we were in New Zealand, and many years ago we saw another one in Norfolk, but these were nothing like Provence.

We were in Malvern researching for the Edward Elgar exhibition when we went into the tourist information shop and I found an advertising leaflet showing the wonderful fields of lavender at the Snowshill Lavender Farm in the Cotswolds, Gloucestershire. I did not even know they were there. We went to find the farm a few weeks later – what a wonderful sight: field upon field of lavender in dark, vivid purple, with rows and rows of flowers. I was in my element, and took many photographs. The farm grows lots of different species of lavender, from white to pale pinks and purples, some of which I now have in my garden. Most of the rows of lavender were immaculate but I liked this photograph best, as it has this beautifully elegant cream grass growing in between the rounded lavender bushes. The main focus is the white house at the end of the lines of lavender, slightly offset to give interest. The rows of lavender bushes and the pathways between them draw your eye to this main focal point.

We have been to the centre many times since that day, and I am looking forward to creating lots of other pictures from the photographs I have taken there. On page 55, you can see a simple lavender picture that I have made ready to demonstrate it at a workshop.

I hope you enjoy stitching this project as much as I did.

1 I enlarged this 10 x 15cm (4 x 6in) photograph to A4, in colour on to photographic paper using the best photographic setting on the photocopier. I then photocopied this on to ordinary photocopy paper using the text setting. I placed a piece of tracing paper over the A4 colour photocopy and traced the main design lines using a mechanical pencil. I then photocopied the tracing twice in black and white, so that I could use the copies as patterns, one for the main pattern and the other for the hedge and house in the background.

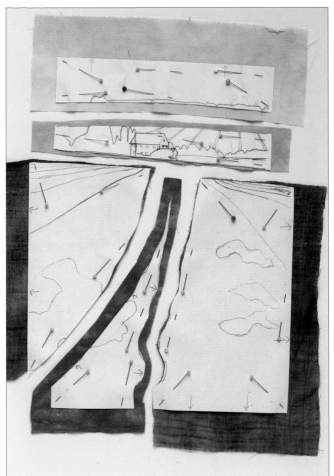

2 Take one piece of the white cotton fabric, place it over the photocopied design lines and put both on a light box. Trace the lines on to the white fabric with a mechanical pencil.

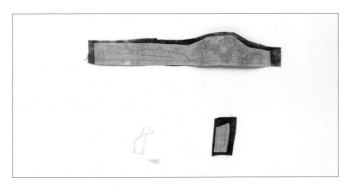

3 Cut out your pattern from the other main design lines photocopy. Write on each section of the pattern either the name or number of each piece for identification. Place the sky pattern on to a pale blue cotton fabric and pin it in place, leaving enough room to add a 5mm (¼in) seam allowance to the lower edge and 2.5cm (1in) to the top and both sides. Cut the sky piece out. Pin the hill pattern on to the pale green space-dyed cotton. Cut it out adding a 5mm (¼in) seam allowance to the top edge and 2.5cm (1in) to both sides. Pin the path pattern on to the brown space-dyed fabric, adding 5mm (¼in) seam allowances to both sides and the top point of the path and 2.5cm (1in) at the bottom and the bottom section outside edge. Cut the path out. Pin the lavender field to purple space-dyed cotton fabric. Cut it out, adding 2.5cm (1in) seam allowances to the sides and bottom.

4 Place the second black and white photocopy face down and trace the hedge outline on to the reverse side to give you a mirror image. Trace this side on to the paper backing of the fusible web. Repeat with the second, more distant hedge (not shown). Repeat again with the house and the roof. Cut out each piece, leaving space all around. Place a piece of baking parchment on the ironing board, take the fusible web hedge piece, remove the paper backing and place sticky side down on the dark green space-dyed fabric. Cover with another piece of baking parchment, place a hot iron on the area, remove it and check that all the edges are bonded, and if not, re-press. Repeat with the other hedge piece. Repeat with the roof section on grey fabric and again with the house on white cotton. Leave to cool then cut carefully around the drawn lines with small sharp-pointed scissors. Leave 2.5cm (1in) seam allowance at the side edges and 5mm (¼in) a the bottom edge of both hedge pieces.

5 Place the white cotton with the pencil guide lines on the table. Remove the pattern from the sky fabric and lay it on the white fabric using the drawn line for guidance. Pin it in place. Repeat with the green field, the path and the lavender. Using matching thread, stitch with a very small stitch on top to tack all the pieces in place. Cover the ironing board with baking parchment and lay the tacked picture face up on top. Remove the backing paper from the hedge sections, lay them in place with the 5mm (¼in) seam allowance under the hill and the lavender field, cover with more baking parchment and press gently with a hot iron. Repeat with the house and roof.

Note
Use the pattern to guide you for the perspective lines: the tractor lines in the background field and the lavender rows in the foreground field.

6 Use the purple crystal organza to cover the lavender field area and pin it in place. Cut out the lavender field area of your paper pattern. Cut one line at a time, starting at the centre. Lay it on your work to give you accurate lines, which is important for showing perspective. Use a small running stitch in purple thread to tack the design lines, using the cut pattern as a guide. Take the white crystal organza, which will give a little sparkle to the sky. Cut out two of each of the cloud shapes. Position the double layer of cloud shapes and tack them with a small running stitch.

Cut narrow strips of dark purple chiffon tapering at one end. Following the perspective lines, lay them on to the shadow sides of the lavender rows as shown.

Cut out small jagged pieces from the green chiffon and distress it with your fingers to gather it and make holes. Pin it in place, following the picture, to represent areas of grass growing between the lavender. Tack it in place. I like the imperfection of the grass, but if you prefer you can leave it out, giving you prefect lines.

Take your second piece of white cotton, lay it on the work surface, lay the wadding on top and your picture right side up on top of the wadding. Pin through all thicknesses. Tack with large stitches using white tacking thread. Work in a grid shape from the centre outwards top to bottom then across the picture from side to side.

7 The stitching starts with the sky. Start to stitch from the centre of the sky outwards, using pale blue viscose thread in straight lines for the clear part. Stitch with white viscose thread in scalloped shapes to represent fluffy clouds. Outline the clouds with the blue to emphasise the shape. Change colours as you work across the picture.

8 Stitch the centre section of the top hedge first, using olive green viscose thread, then the left- and right-hand sections using a darker green thread. Add machine stitching for the skeletal tree branches as you go.

9 Using your paper scissors, cut along the tractor lines on your paper pattern. Leave a small section at the bottom uncut so that you do not lose the tiny pieces. Place the

pattern on your work and pin it in place. Machine stitch with the darker green thread, stitching two lines close together to represent the tractor lines, following the angle on the paper pattern. Remove the paper pattern one section at a time, then stitch the field lines with pale green random thread. Work your way across, changing colours as required. Repeat on the other side.

10 For the house roof, change to an appliqué or open-toed machine foot, lift the dogteeth and set the machine to a very narrow zigzag satin stitch. You do not need a wide satin stitch because the roof has been attached with fusible web. Using matching light brown viscose thread, stitch round the edge of the roof and chimney. Change machine settings to straight stitch and stitch the horizontal lines for the lines of the tiles. Change to a free machine embroidery foot, drop the dogteeth and thread the machine with white viscose thread. Stitch the white section of the house with straight lines. Change to pale brown thread, stitch in a suggestion of windows and the down pipe.

11 Machine the front hedge with medium green thread. Work with circular movements to represent the foliage. Add shadows with a darker green thread. Stitch the tall conifers with dark green thread. Work the lines across to represent the grass and hedges in dark and light greens on the right-hand side. Stitch in the other buildings. Machine the roofs with the light brown thread in straight stitch. Leave no gaps so that it covers the hedge that may have been stitched in these areas. Now with the white, fill in the area for the walls of the buildings.

12 To begin the lavender field, use your paper pattern and your tacking lines for guidance. Working from the centre, stitch the left-hand side of the pathway in dark purple, working tight circular movements for about 5cm (2in). Stitch the right-side in pale lilac. Approximately 3cm (1¼in) down, introduce the pale green on the left-hand side. Do not be tempted to complete the pathway; you must work only 5cm (2in), then stop.

Now start to work the lavender rows, working outwards. Change the machine thread as required. Look at the picture and arch your stitching to give curves to the top of the lavender bushes. The dark purple lines lie on your tacked stitched guidelines. Work your way gradually outwards, making sure you do not pleat your fabric. If you find this difficult, work only a short distance at a time. Continue working in this way, always going back to the centre and then working out to the sides. The pathway begins to change and you can see the soil, so stitch this with light brown thread.

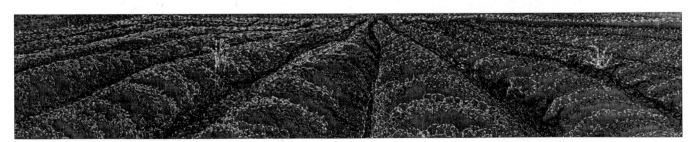

13 Half way down the field, as the lavender gets nearer to the viewer, change the stitching to a spiked straight stitch. Gradually add the grass, using light, medium and dark green when you reach the areas of green chiffon. Make the grass in the rows taller and the grass in the path shorter. In the foreground, create more detail on the lavender flowers, and stitch some of the flower heads with a side-to-side motion. I also used pale pink and white to highlight the flower heads. On the lower part of the path, make the stitched circles larger to look like pebbles. Stitch the left-hand side with dark purple and brown. Stitch the large pale grasses with ecru and cream, curving some of them over to give a soft effect. Stitch the seed heads on each stem with straight stitch, narrow at the top and wider at the bottom. Finally, sign your name in the cream thread.

Overleaf
The finished picture.

The Old Wood Shed

This picture is of my wood shed, which is at least seventy years old. It has such character even though the door has gone, the tin roof is rusty and the walls are falling away. It has been home to chickens and our first dog Bobby had his kennel in it. The birds, especially robins, love to hop in and out of the huge ivy bush which overlaps the roof. My granddaughters pick blackberries from the brambles at the side of the shed.

I used blue and white space-dyed cotton for the sky and orange space-dyed cotton for the background trees, overlaid with small pieces of orange, green and yellow chiffon and organza. The trees were then heavily machine embroidered with viscose thread. I used green space-dyed cotton for the ivy bush, overlaid with small pieces of scrim, chiffon and organza for the dense foliage. This was also machine embroidered. The conifer on the right was created from blue-green space-dyed cotton overlaid with chiffon and scrim. The trunk and branches were made from purple shades of space-dyed cotton. Machine embroidery was used to extend the tips of the small branches beyond the green fabric to give detail. The sheds were done with space-dyed cottons with scrim laid on to the wooden walls to give the ageing effect. The detail was created using machine embroidery. The grass is space-dyed green cotton with machine stitched detail. The tubs were created with blue-grey cotton using fusible web to attach and prevent fraying, with machine-stitched detail. The hanging basket was machine stitched, and the wood inside the shed was machine stitched in greens and browns.

Naas House

Naas House is such a lovely grand, imposing building, and it is very unusual with the tower on top of the house. The first time I saw it was around 1961 when I was studying at Lydney School Of Art. Mr Prothero, my Art lecturer, had taken students into the grounds of Naas Farm for an outdoor painting lesson – I think this was probably my first outdoor oil painting. The house is thought to have been built in the early 1600s. It remains much as it was recorded to have looked in 1720. During the Civil War it was a garrison for the Parliamentarians. From the tower they would have had a good view of the River Severn, and it would have been possible to see any ships sailing up towards the docks.

When I took my painting home, my father was delighted; he said the Biddle family who now owned the farm were relations of his and he proudly took it to show them.

I have worked this picture as a copy of my painting rather than of the more up to date photographs that I have taken. The paint on the house is now peeling and practically gone and the huge trees behind it have been cut down, so it looks a little sad.

The sky is from one piece of blue and white space-dyed fabric. It was stitched with light, medium and dark blue and white viscose thread with a straight stitch in a side-to-side movement, and I blended the colours as I worked. The trees, wall, hedges and the buildings are held in place with fusible web, and the details were then stitched in. The fields are in two pieces of fabric with the road fabric placed in between them, and these were all finally machined in place. The fence posts are graduated in height, showing the perspective, and they are also spaced so that the gap between each one gets smaller as they go into the distance.

Index

autumn 14, 25, 44, 48, 53, 72–73, 78–85, 87, 107

beads 14, 54, 56, 60, 70
building 17, 18, 19, 28, 58, 59, 62, 66, 70, 122, 126

cloud 40, 41, 42, 43, 53, 58, 68, 117, 120, 121
composition 18, 30, 32, 88

design 6, 15, 16–21, 30, 79, 83, 89, 108, 109, 118, 119, 120
distance 7, 12, 17, 18, 36, 40, 44, 45, 48, 52, 53, 54, 56, 57, 58–59, 60, 62, 66, 68, 70
dyeing 7, 8, 10, 14, 22–29, 32, 33, 43, 55, 56, 65, 68, 70, 72, 74
    procion dyes 7, 8, 22
    space-dyed/space-dyeing 7, 10, 14, 15, 21, 25, 40, 41, 42, 43, 45, 46, 47, 48, 50, 52, 53, 55, 56, 57, 59, 62, 65, 66, 67, 68, 70, 72, 74, 78, 79, 83, 87, 88, 96, 97, 98, 107, 108, 117, 119, 125, 126

fabric 6, 7, 10–11, 12, 13, 14, 15, 20, 21, 22, 23, 24, 25, 26, 28, 30, 31, 32, 33, 34, 37, 43, 45, 48, 50, 52, 54, 55, 56, 57, 58, 64, 65, 66, 67, 70, 72, 74, 78, 79, 80, 81, 83, 87, 88, 89, 90, 91, 96, 98, 99, 100, 107, 108, 109, 111, 112, 119, 120, 122, 126
    calico 10, 22, 23, 47, 65, 117
    chiffon 10, 11, 40, 43, 47, 48, 51, 54, 68, 70, 72, 74, 78, 88, 90, 96, 117, 118, 120, 123, 125
    cotton 7, 10, 11, 21, 22, 23, 25, 26, 28, 31, 32, 40, 41, 42, 43, 45, 46, 47, 50, 52, 53, 54, 55, 56, 57, 59, 62, 65, 66, 67, 70, 78, 79, 81, 83, 88, 89, 90, 96, 97, 98, 108, 109, 117, 119, 120, 125
    cotton lace 11, 14, 22, 23, 24, 26, 55
    cotton lawn 10, 26
    crepe 10, 11, 22, 23
    gauze 10, 28
    muslin 10, 21, 23, 31, 32
    organza 7, 10, 11, 14, 31, 35, 40, 41, 42, 43, 44, 45, 46, 52, 56, 59, 70, 72, 77, 78, 96, 98, 99, 108, 109, 110, 117, 118, 120, 125
    polyester/cotton 11, 22, 23, 28, 32
    scrim 10, 11, 21, 23, 28, 31, 32, 33, 38, 48, 50, 53, 55, 65, 67, 78, 87, 90, 117, 125
    silk 10, 11, 22, 28, 43, 47, 54, 57, 97
    velvet 10, 11, 28, 43
    viscose 11, 22, 23, 28, 48, 52, 56, 70, 88, 90
fibres 6, 10, 11, 22, 28, 117

field 6, 14, 21, 30, 31, 32, 36, 37, 38, 53, 54, 55, 56, 58, 59, 60, 62, 63, 70, 74, 107, 108, 119, 120, 122, 123, 126
flowers 14, 16, 17, 21, 31, 32, 37, 38, 42, 47, 54–57, 60, 88–97
    bluebell 18, 48, 50, 54, 57, 61, 68, 87
    lavender 14, 41, 55, 60, 66, 118–124
    poppy/poppies 14, 21, 31, 41, 54, 56, 59, 60, 70
foliage 48, 54, 81, 88, 122, 125
foreground 7, 16, 17, 18, 21, 32, 38, 45, 53, 54, 56, 58, 60, 62, 65, 68, 70, 72, 74, 79, 82, 83, 90, 91, 99, 104, 107, 108, 109, 110, 123
forest 6, 16, 77
Forest of Dean 6, 60, 68, 70, 72, 74, 78
fusible web 7, 15, 31, 33, 54, 57, 78, 79, 80, 83, 117, 118, 119, 121, 125, 126

grass 21, 31, 32, 38, 55, 57, 60, 61, 62, 83, 117, 118, 120, 122, 123

highlight 21, 36, 38, 48, 52–53, 56, 59, 64, 66, 81, 87, 96, 123
hill 6, 7, 16, 21, 25, 30, 31, 35, 36, 43, 45, 52–53, 58, 68, 70, 74, 107, 109, 117, 119
horizon 17, 55, 59

lace 14, 90, 92
lake 6, 16, 18, 44, 45, 98–107
light source 17, 19, 74

mountains 16, 18, 25, 40, 44, 46, 52–53, 98–107, 108, 111, 112, 117

pattern 13, 15, 17, 31, 56, 78, 79, 80, 89, 98, 99, 108, 109, 118, 119, 120, 122
pebble 19, 47, 64, 104, 117, 123
perspective 18, 58, 60, 62, 74, 83, 91, 113, 120, 126
photograph 6, 15, 16, 17, 18, 30, 40, 43, 48, 51, 58, 65, 68, 70, 72, 74, 78, 87, 88, 89, 98, 107, 108, 109, 117, 118

reflection 12, 21, 44, 45, 46, 47, 51, 72, 109, 111, 112
ribbon 14, 108, 113
rock 44, 52, 64–65, 98, 99, 103, 104, 112, 117

sea 7, 52, 59
sewing machine 13, 20, 31, 34
shadow 11, 17, 19, 21, 30, 35, 36, 37, 38, 40, 47, 48, 50, 51, 52, 56, 57, 62, 64, 66, 70, 74, 81, 82, 83, 87, 94, 96, 98, 99, 104, 117, 122
sky/skies 7, 20, 21, 25, 31, 34, 35, 37, 40–43, 42, 45, 46, 48, 53, 55, 59, 68, 70, 74, 79, 81, 82, 89, 90, 98, 99, 100, 103, 108, 109, 111, 112, 117, 119, 120, 121, 125
spring 68–69

summer 31, 40, 41, 42, 45, 60, 70–71
sunset 14, 16, 40, 42, 43, 44, 46, 52, 108–115

techniques
    appliqué 7, 10, 15, 48, 52, 53, 54, 56, 58, 68, 70, 72, 77, 88, 91, 118, 121
    continuous swirl pattern 41, 42, 90
    distress(ing) 10, 21, 32, 40, 43, 47, 51, 53, 65, 67, 68, 87, 90, 96, 117, 120
    free machine embroidery/stitching 13, 34, 48, 51, 68, 70, 72, 77, 78, 81, 88, 90, 91, 98, 100, 107, 108, 111, 112, 114, 118, 121
    French knots 12, 21, 38, 54, 56, 60, 70
    fusible web appliqué 33, 41, 44, 58, 60, 66, 67
    hand embroidery/stitching 10, 13, 20, 33, 54, 56, 62, 70, 74, 99, 111
    machine stitching 7, 10, 11, 12, 20, 21, 35, 38, 41, 42, 43, 44, 48, 52, 53, 54, 56, 57, 58, 59, 64, 65, 66, 67, 68, 70, 74, 81, 87, 117, 121, 125
    outline 50, 65, 94, 102, 121
    tack(ing) 34, 80, 81, 89, 90, 91, 98, 99, 108, 110, 113, 120, 122
    torn strip 7, 32, 41, 42, 48, 52, 53, 57, 59, 68, 70, 77, 87, 107
    turned edge 53, 111
texture 6, 10, 17, 20, 28, 32, 42, 48, 50, 67, 90, 117
thread 6, 7, 10, 12, 13, 20, 22, 23, 24, 26, 28, 31, 33, 34, 35, 36, 37, 38, 42, 59, 62, 80, 81, 82, 83, 90, 92, 93, 94, 99, 100, 111, 112, 114, 117, 120, 122
    machine-embroidery 12, 56, 78, 88, 98, 118
    metallic 12, 13, 44, 72, 78, 104, 117
    six-strand embroidery 12, 21, 54, 62, 63, 70
    viscose 12, 20, 31, 33, 42, 43, 44, 46, 47, 48, 51, 52, 56, 68, 74, 78, 87, 88, 91, 98, 108, 111, 117, 118, 125, 126
tree 7, 17, 18, 19, 21, 25, 30, 31, 32, 33, 36, 37, 43, 44, 45, 46, 47, 48–51, 55, 56, 57, 58, 59, 60, 67, 68, 70, 72, 74, 77, 79, 80, 81, 82, 83, 87, 90, 91, 96, 102, 107, 125, 126

wadding (batting) 11, 13, 20, 31, 34, 47, 65, 78, 81, 88, 90, 98, 99, 108, 110, 118, 120
water 7, 12, 14, 25, 44–47, 51, 61, 62, 65, 72, 74, 77, 96, 99, 102, 103, 104, 107, 108, 109, 110, 111, 112, 114, 117
winter 42, 48, 58, 63, 74–75
wood/woodland 16, 18, 31, 48–51, 54, 57, 68, 77, 78–85, 87

yarn 14, 47, 117